Leadership in Times of Stress and Change

Seven Skills for Gaining Trust and Inspiring Confidence

Harry L. Woodward, Ph.D.
Mark J. Tager, M.D.

WorkSkills-LifeSkills

WorkSkills LifeSkills

For more information:
www.workskills-lifeskills.com
or toll-free
1-877-WORK567 (967-5567)

WorkSkills-LifeSkills
9237 Regents Rd., Suite 126
La Jolla, CA 92037
Phone: 858-202-1491
Fax: 858-202-1497

Email:
mtager@workskills-lifeskills.com

Woodward Learning International, Inc.

For more information:
www.woodlearn.com
Woodward Learning
International, Inc.
4905 13th Avenue South
Minneapolis, MN 55417
Phone: 612-824-1410
Fax: 612-822-6777

Email:
hlw@woodlearn.com

TABLE OF CONTENTS

ACKNOWLEDGMENTS

One of our favorite exercises is to ask workshop participants to draw a picture of their organization. The vast majority of drawings look like either organizational charts or pyramids. In the pyramid model, leaders at various levels spend time and energy being responsible to those above them. The power of this exercise comes when the pyramid is inverted and each level of management focuses—not on being responsible—but being responsive, to the larger group that is now above them.

In crafting *Leadership in Times of Stress and Change*, we've tried to apply this principle and create a program that better meets the needs of our audience. We've inverted the pyramid by involving our associates in defining and shaping the content. Now it's time to thank them for their help. The largest group is composed of our colleagues at the Society for Human Resource Management. For their input, feedback, and support, our gratitude goes out to:

Belinda Anderson	James Imler
Kathleen Anderson	Carolyn Lawson
Dennis Briscoe	Niki J. Lee
Linda K. Buck	Debra Lindh
Jeffrey Chambers	Cynthia L. Mercer
Mike Colon	Jean Miller
Craig A. Copper	Cynthia Palomo
Stephanie Curran	Tina Pocrnich
Vickie Eads	John Prange
Shawn Featherston	Leda M. Quiros-Weed
John Hale	Beth M. Rogers
Jon Hoag	Roger D. Sommer
Maudie Holm	

A number of our colleagues at the International Association of Business Communicators also provided input into the chapter "Communicate with Credibility." Members of the Los Angeles and Orange County groups were wonderfully responsive, providing not just big-picture feedback, but also nitty-gritty tips and techniques. Special thanks go out to Chris Cabrera and Rich Nemec, who doggedly pursued us to make certain we received their feedback.

We'd also like to acknowledge a number of exceptional leaders with whom we have had the pleasure of working. These people serve as our mentors in handling change and stress with competence and grace. Sharing our belief in the importance of building better leaders, healthier people, and stronger organizations, we are indebted to Ralph Bahna, Lynne Bardy, John Berg, Sam Bresler, John Bunyan, Cindy Dulon, Phyllis Huckabee, Jim Jameson, Dr. David Lawrence, DeBorah Lenchard, Teri Louden, Hawk McIntosh, Virgil Mette, Dick Osgood, and Joyce Rowland.

As always, we wish to thank our wives, Carol Tager and Mary Woodward, for their ongoing support, their perspectives and insights into the world of change and stress, and their valuable suggestions to the manuscript.

Finally, there's our wonderful team who worked hard to make *Leadership in Times of Stress and Change* a reality. Our gratitude goes out to Norm Nouskajian for legal assistance, Nancy Van Allen for design and illustration, Kathy Meunier for copy editing, and Corinna Buchholz for her editorial acumen.

HAVE IT YOUR WAY

Welcome to *Leadership in Times of Stress and Change: Seven Skills for Gaining Trust and Inspiring Confidence.* For the past twenty-five years, we've had the privilege of working with organizations and individuals as they wrestled with the challenges of changing work environments. We've seen firsthand the effects that the resulting stress has on people: how it either erodes health, self-confidence, and performance; or brings out the best in employees and teams. What follows are the nuggets that we have gleaned from this work, presented as straightforward, practical tools that leaders at any organizational level can use to help reach their personal and organizational goals.

There are several ways to use this book. The first is to explore the seven areas of importance, chapters 1 through 7. As you do so, we will be asking you to make some changes, try new techniques, and possibly adopt a different attitude and philosophy about your role in working with others. For those with less time, you may wish to skim the introduction, take the inventory, and then concentrate on those key areas that will provide you with the greatest payoff.

You can also take this program one step further. *Leadership in Times of Stress and Change* features a comprehensive online inventory, as well as an online and in-person training program. For those of you who would like a more in-depth approach, we encourage you to contact us through the information on the copyright page.

As John F. Kennedy once wrote, "Leadership and learning are indispensable to each other." In the next several chapters, you'll learn the skills to become a better leader, and also gain knowledge about yourself and your organization through the process of leading.

— Mark & Harry

THE LEADERSHIP CHALLENGE

Every business leader is aware of the competition, the other organizations with similar products and services. But there's another type of competition facing today's leaders—one that is often overlooked—competition for the energy, loyalty, and focus of your people.

It's fierce competition. Why? Because we have entered an era of constant change and increasing stress. We live in a 24/7 world where we are constantly bombarded by emails, phone calls, faxes, and overnight deliveries. Television, radio, and the Internet bring global problems to our doorsteps every day. The drive for improved productivity has resulted in increasing workloads and shrinking staffs. Commutes have increased. Tempers have shortened. In the wake of terrorist attacks, uncertainty pervades the nation. Downturns, mergers, and acquisitions have made reorganization more the norm than the exception.

It is in this milieu that you, the leader, continue your quest to positively influence your people. To do this, to gain mindshare, you'll need to get them to put aside unnecessary concerns, distractions, and harmful emotions to focus on the work at hand. But how do you do this?

It would be nice if there were a recipe or whole cookbook outlining a step-by-step process that would guarantee your success. Chances are, whoever produced this cookbook would market it as the "new and improved" leadership product. We believe that very little is new in leadership. The tools are the same as ever. Leaders do two things. They provide direction to their people: addressing the who, what, where, when, and how of the situation. And they provide support in the form of praise, encouragement, listening, feedback, reinforcement, and self-disclosure.

What *is* new in leadership, however, is the need to adjust your style so that you are providing people with the right mixture of direction and support in these challenging times. This involves both a recognition that things are different and a willingness to change how you approach people and situations. To get the right leadership combination, it is helpful to acknowledge the following:

You Already Have Established Leadership Habits

These leadership traits are the result of three factors that shape what you do:

- **Natural tendencies.** Those of you who have taken a personality-based assessment such as the Myers-Briggs Type Inventory, the PowerSource Profile, or the Social Style Inventory are already aware of some of your inherent preferences such as how you acquire and process information, your need for closure, or your tendency toward intro- or extroversion. A number of your management strengths and weaknesses find their roots in these natural preferences.

- **Your work experience.** At this point in your career, you've gone through your share of training courses.

You've gained tools and have been influenced by leaders and mentors. You have also observed and been part of change efforts in your company that turned out well, and others that did not. Your style is strongly influenced by these experiences; there is a natural comfort in using solutions that worked well in the past, even though the new context may demand a different approach.

- **Your attitudes and beliefs.** Many factors contribute to developing your views on life and your beliefs. These include parental, peer, and religious influences, early upbringing, and personal accomplishments and setbacks. All of these elements combine to determine whether you see yourself as being in control of life's situations or limited by circumstances, whether you look at change as a problem or a challenge, and whether you have the necessary commitment to see things through.

Everyone has a different combination of experiences and philosophies. This combination is a mixed bag, with its own levels of appropriateness for the situation at hand. Some aspects of your leadership style will be effective most of the time, other parts rarely. Some techniques are fine for stable environments, but totally inappropriate for changing ones. Understanding your unique blend of leadership habits is an important place to start, and you can begin this process by taking the Leadership Change Inventory in the following chapter.

But before you explore personal aspects of your leadership style, let's take a look at some of the traits that exceptional leaders share.

UNDERSTANDING LEADERSHIP

Let's face it, when things are relatively stable—when market conditions are healthy, when production of goods and services is running smoothly, when morale is high—most organizations don't really need leaders. They need managers or supervisors who follow the rules and established processes of Basic Management 101 and who are smart enough to avoid screwing things up.

When things get tough, though, when the necessity for rules diminishes, organizations need people willing to lead with three key attributes:

- **Flexibility:** the willingness and capacity to do things differently, to take the risks involved, and to admit to a level of uncertainty.
- **Empathy:** the ability to put yourself in the shoes of your employees, to really know and feel what each is going through.
- **Trustworthiness:** the congruence of your thoughts, feelings, and actions, expressed in a manner that results in others finding you credible.

These three attributes are an integral part of the seven skills presented in *Leadership in Times of Stress and Change*. Empathy ("Take the LEAP with Your People") and trustworthiness ("Communicating with Credibility") are discussed in great detail. Let's take a closer look at flexibility, especially in light of the recognition that each leader has established habits.

Do Less, Be More

Our experience has led us to believe that most managers and supervisors are doers. They solve problems by taking charge, rallying the troops and directing their activities. Our Western management system places a high value on action and on "hard skills" such as measurement, analytics, appraisals, objectives, and tasks. These are all important items, in fact they are crucial for performance. The problem emerges when leaders rely heavily on them in changing times, when a different skillset is required.

In times of stress and change, the competencies required for effectiveness are the leadership skills that involve spending additional time with people, not telling them what to do, but instead listening more. Rather than issuing directives and expecting immediate compliance, you may need to go over the same issue many times, from many viewpoints. Moving forward in changing times means first stepping back long enough to understand how people are reacting, then crafting an other-centered strategy to move them along. These people-centered skills may seem like a waste of time, especially when time is in short supply. Or they may appear to be a weak replacement for "real" action. Yet paying attention to these skills of involvement with your employees can be the most important and strongest leadership task to accomplish during stressful times. As we'll see below, it makes a big difference in the health and productivity of your people and your company.

What You Do Makes a Difference

In our training program, we conduct an exercise that drives home the important influence that leaders have on their people's confidence, commitment, and well-being. We ask workshop participants to think about the *worst boss* they've ever had. What did that boss do and how did those actions affect the participant? After generating a list of actions and consequences, we go on to ask people to generate a list for the *best boss* they've ever worked for; what did the best boss do and how did it make them feel? The comparison is striking. "Bad bosses" erode confidence and create climates of fear; they whittle away at self-esteem and put people in lose-lose situations. People who believe their bosses are bad become depressed, anxious, or angry; they don't sleep at night, blood pressures rise and muscle tension increases. Ulcers, nervous tics, rashes, and headaches become commonplace. The good boss, on the other hand, creates a state of confidence and commitment in people. People who have experienced good bosses often feel mentally tougher and more willing to take risks for the company. They are loyal, committed, and will go that extra mile. When their boss helps them get through tough times, they reap a sense of personal growth and accomplishment.

As authors, consultants, and seminar leaders, we're always on the lookout for examples of positive change experiences. In the course of writing this book, numerous colleagues shared with us stories of bosses, mentors, and coworkers who had "done it right"—who had gained the trust of their workforce and inspired performance during stressful times. You'll find some of this correspondence in the appendix. What's notable is the passion with which people wrote about their "best bosses," even after many years had elapsed.

Change can be difficult, and leaders with great influence wield a double-edged sword over their employees. They can make the process even more difficult by clamming up and charging ahead without acknowledging people's fears and feelings. But good leaders can also learn to make the process less painful—and their employees and the company can be stronger for it.

In Stressful Times, Give Up the Expectation That People Will Respond Rationally

When people are shocked, two opposite, "irrational" emotional states tend to prevail. The first is *withdrawal.* They shut down emotionally. They become incapacitated by sadness. Their body language is closed and protective. They avoid eye contact and turn inward to avoid any more stimulation. In the second state, rather than withdrawing, they become *hypervigilant.* They are completely on edge. Little things set them off. Their body goes into hyperdrive as they become more frantic and frustrated. This frustration is often expressed as anger or in unfocused, frenetic action that accomplishes little. To complicate the issue, it is normal for people responding to significant change to vacillate between the two states, at times being withdrawn, at other times being hyperactive. While the external expression is different, the end result is the same. When people react in these ways, they aren't acting rationally because they are having difficulty receiving and interpreting information:

- **Perception.** They miss important clues from the environment. When in withdrawal, people shut out the very information that could help them move through the change. In the hyperactive state, they are so overloaded and unfocused that they can't attend to the information, and therefore it fails to register.

- **Processing.** In the hypervigilant state, every input is viewed as a potential threat. With the body in its "fight or flight" alarm reaction, processing becomes distorted. Hypervigilants will misinterpret words and gestures, often attaching false or inappropriate meaning to harmless phrases or body language. For those in the withdrawal state, it is almost as if the information is being filtered through molasses. Things remain fuzzy and unclear.

By understanding that change can produce seemingly nonsensical responses in rational individuals, leaders can better predict employees' fears and address their concerns.

LET GO OF THE NEED FOR CERTAINTY

In your business career, how many times have you been in a situation where you were totally certain of your goal and completely confident in your (and your people's) ability to get there? Most of us can count these moments on one or two hands. This is the Valhalla of leadership. We long to get to this place, even if we know our stay will be short-lived. Many managers idealize this state and remember when, in years past, they washed up on its shores, when things were normal and controllable, when the pace of change was moderate and people acted predictably.

We liken these moments to gazing at a calm, waveless ocean where nary a ripple breaks the mirror-like smoothness. We all know these moments are fleeting, the tides and waves will exert their inevitable pulls and disturb this reflection. At times, there will be rough seas, strong tides, and unpredictable swells. Navigating these waters will present a new set of challenges, affecting both your confidence and certainty and your people's as well. This dynamic is shown on the Marhari Grid* below, and reflected in the representative statements in each of the quadrants.

The Marhari Grid

Let's take a closer look at the quadrants formed by this grid.

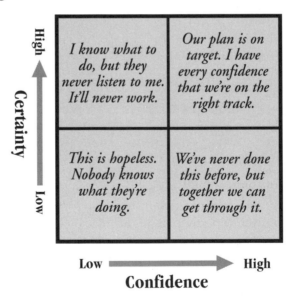

* We admit, we couldn't resist the play on words. One of the most widely known insight tools, developed in the fifties by Joseph Luft and Harry Ingham, is the Johari Window. The term was created by merging the first names of its originators.

High confidence, high certainty

You are operating in a normal, stable, but fleeting environment, marked by two states: high levels of confidence and high levels of certainty. You know what to do, the course of action is clear, and you are confident in your plan and approach. In a stable environment, planning provides and supports these feelings. It works well when you have all the information, the situation is proceeding incrementally, and your people are all acting rationally. This is reflected in the general sentiment that "we're on track and we're gonna reach our goal."

Low confidence, low certainty

Now let's look at the opposite quadrant, low confidence, low certainty. This point represents the lowest end of the scale in morale or work climate surveys. People are unsure and afraid. When a high percentage of people in the organization share this viewpoint, it is often an indication that leadership development is bankrupt. The organization has failed to invest in training that empowers employees, builds strong, functional teams, and values participation and innovation. Now when the organization needs to "go to the bank," when it asks people to sacrifice for the company, there's little goodwill upon which to draw.

Low confidence, high certainty

This state is most common when people have not been allowed to participate in decisions that affect them. Their contributions and ideas have not been valued, even though they may be the people closest to the customer or the problem. There is an undercurrent of resentment and resignation. After reorganizations, these are often the people who have "quit but stayed." They bide their time and stop contributing because experience has told them that their input will not be valued.

High confidence, low certainty

When we ask managers whether it is their job to be

confident and *certain*, most say yes. How about confident and *uncertain*, we ask. Most reply that uncertainty is a sign of weakness, that leaders should project an aura of definitiveness.

Yet uncertainty is a large part of change—an aspect that can be exciting and rewarding if approached with honesty. It takes a strong leader to say, "I'm not sure how we're going to get where we need to be, but I am confident that we will come up with a plan to get there." The goal of leadership in changing times is to find comfort in being *confident but uncertain*. In fact, this is the only position that will be viewed as credible by those who work for and with you.

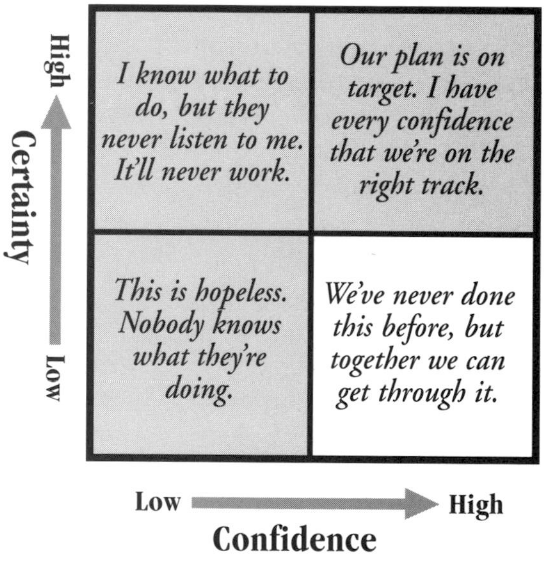

	Low ⟶ Confidence ⟶ High
High *(Certainty)*	*I know what to do, but they never listen to me. It'll never work.*	*Our plan is on target. I have every confidence that we're on the right track.*
Low *(Certainty)*	*This is hopeless. Nobody knows what they're doing.*	*We've never done this before, but together we can get through it.*

Certainty (vertical axis, Low to High) — Confidence (horizontal axis, Low to High)

I'm *Sure* I Don't Know Exactly How We'll Get There

Being confident in uncertain times and situations presupposes that you are willing to relinquish a certain measure of control and to seek, value, and use the energy and input of your team. Managers who are willing to admit they don't have all the answers often feel an incredible sense of relief that the burden is off their shoulders and shared by the team. The confidence is in the we, not the me. Together we can do it. And employees are willing to work harder for a goal, even if it's uncertain, if you've been upfront about your own limitations and they've had input in the process.

At this point in our workshops, after we have introduced the idea of confidence and uncertainty as an ideal, many managers raise the what ifs:

- **What if my team doesn't have the necessary skills?**
- **What if my people don't view me (or another leader) as credible in the current climate?**
- **What if people are angry or upset because of circumstances that can't be controlled?**
- **If I've been a highly directive leader, are you telling me I need to have people invested in the process and participating, that I need to change overnight?**

Our response to these questions is: Never underestimate people's capacity to rise to the challenge. Tough times can bring out the best in everyone. When you create a climate that is inclusive, open, and affirming, many people are willing to give you the benefit of the doubt, to wipe the slate clean of past grievances and work with, as opposed to against, you. For those with doubts in the power of teams, we encourage you to reflect on the words of Margaret Mead:

Never doubt that a small group of thoughtful, committed citizens can change the world. Indeed it is the only thing that ever has.

A final note before we move on. Throughout this book we talk a lot about stress as a result of change. Any time managers motivate their workforce, they are adding

19

stress to increase performance. And any time we want to make personal changes—to work harder for a promotion, to take classes to educate ourselves, even to make the decision to have and raise children—we are adding additional stress to our lives. As change leaders, we realize that stress is often a positive motivator for growth and accomplishment. In this book, however, when we talk about stress, we will more often than not refer to its negative consequences—strain and distress—because these are the perceptions that most people have of stress during challenging times. It is our goal in this book to minimize the adverse results of stress and strain and make change a more manageable and positive experience.

YOUR GUIDEBOOK TO CHANGE

Throughout this introduction, we've presented the idea that the goal of a great change leader is not to pretend to know all the answers, but rather to have and inspire confidence through honesty. We, too, don't claim to have all the right answers. Instead, we're offering you a guidebook to the seven major stages of a positive change, written by people who've been through the process and helped others along the journey. This is not a book of tactics, but rather a collection of templates. It does not deal with providing direction for common job tasks. Other books detail specific elements of supervision and how to provide the right mix of instruction and praise. What we offer instead is insight into the process of change. It's up to you to decide how much time and attention to devote to various parts of the trip, whether it's better to occasionally skip ahead or veer off course. Your specific path through stressful times depends on many variables: the amount and type of information available, the degree of emotional disturbance a situation could cause, and your comfort and ability with various skills.

Our guidebook to change begins with you, in both the Leadership Change Inventory, which will test your comfort levels with certain aspects of change, and through chapter 1: "Look Within Before Venturing Out." Chapter 2, "Clarify the New Context," addresses the importance of not only knowing where you are at the beginning of your trip, but also of communicating this location to others and seeking their input. Chapter 3, "Set a Direction, Even Though It's Likely to Change," discusses the difference in value between *making* and *following* a plan. "Communicate with Credibility," chapter 4, explores the importance of self-disclosure in inspiring trust and addresses the question of how much information is too much to share.

Next is "Take the LEAP with Your People." Think of this as your bungee-jumping excursion. You may be ready to dive off a cliff into change, but you have to make sure that your team members are with you, that someone has checked your ropes and calculated the distance of your jump. To make the leap with your people, you'll need to (L)isten, (E)mpathize, (A)sk, and (P)ropose, rather than charging ahead and ignoring resistance. In chapter 6, "Remember, There's Always One More Way to Look at a Situation," we attempt to demystify creativity, offering numerous techniques and procedures for forming new solutions. In our final area of importance, "Keep Balance in Mind," we offer suggestions for keeping your personal health and enthusiasm high as you go through the change process along with your people.

We've tried to make the book as easy to read and jargon-free as possible. Those of you who want to know more can find supporting studies and research in the appendix. There is one statistic, however, which deals with the magnitude of the disconnect between employers and employees and gets at the crux of the issue, that we have to share up-front. In several recent studies, more than 90 percent of employees listed trust as an important issue for retention in their workplace, while only one-third of those surveyed felt that they currently had a high level of trust within their organization. At the same time, only 6 percent of human resource managers listed a lack of trust as one of the main reasons why employees left. It is this schism that we address in *Leadership in Times of Stress and Change*. How can we gain the trust of our people? How can we inspire confidence and performance during stressful times?

And so we say bon voyage! Being a leader in times of stress and change can be a difficult, frustrating process, but also one that offers great rewards as well as challenges. Go ahead now and take the inventory in the next chapter and see how ready you are for the journey, as well as areas that can use some improvement.

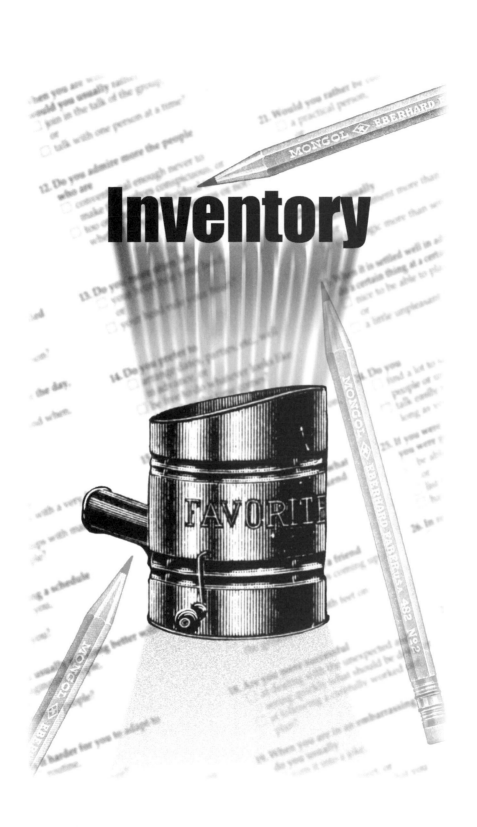

Inventory

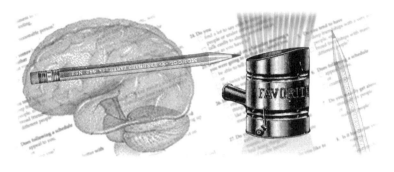

LEADERSHIP CHANGE INVENTORY

Before moving into the content and skills offered in *Leadership in Times of Stress and Change*, we would like you to assess your own *readiness for change*. This inventory provides you with feedback in six key areas. It is an abbreviated version of the comprehensive online Leadership Change Inventory.

To understand how the assessment works, take a look at the following sample question:

When introducing change to people in an organization, I would initially:

Review the changes and encourage people to express their issues and concerns.	1 2 3 4	Explain the organizational and personal benefits of the change and ask for support.

Both of these responses are correct in the sense that both can lead to constructive results in a changing environment. The key word in this question is "initially." The question is asking: What would you do first?

If you felt *strongly* that to review the changes and allow people to express their concerns is the best first step, you would select option 1. If you felt *moderately*

25

about that response as a first step, you would select option 2.

If you felt *moderately* that explaining the benefits of the change and asking for support is the best first step, you would select option 3. If you felt *strongly* about that response, you would select option 4.

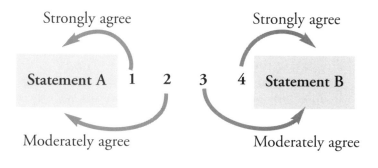

Strongly agree · Strongly agree · Statement A · 1 · 2 · 3 · 4 · Statement B · Moderately agree · Moderately agree

DIRECTIONS

In order for this assessment to be of the most use for you:

- **Read the questions carefully.**
- **Answer honestly.**

This is a self-scoring instrument designed to give you candid feedback. Don't look for the "right" answer. For example, let's say that in reading one of the questions, it strikes you that one of the options is clearly "better"— or the answer you think we're looking for.

Resist the impulse to automatically select that option. Rather, answer honestly from your own experience. *What would you actually do in that situation; how would you really respond?*

Only in this way can you give yourself clear feedback on how effective your attitudes and practices can be in a changing environment.

Are you ready? Please begin. Read the items carefully and circle your choices.

1. If I was experiencing concerns about something I had to communicate to others, I would:

Want to prevent these feelings and thoughts from getting in the way of what I was saying.   **1 2 3 4**   Make sure that what I said basically matched what I was thinking and feeling.

2. Regarding the role of self-reflection—that is, the process of identifying and evaluating what the change will mean to me personally—I would probably:

Self-reflect—then assess the environment.   **1 2 3 4**   Assess the environment and concerns—then self-reflect.

3. In times of rapid change, the organization should address pressing issues by initially identifying:

Outcomes, direction, and actions.   **1 2 3 4**   Goals, plans, and tactics.

4. On receiving new information about current changes, I would:

Use the information as a basis for generating ideas and options.   **1 2 3 4**   Examine the information for its implications for our organization.

27

5. When dealing with the needs of people who are wrestling with the issues of change, I would first try to:

| Legitimize their concerns and discover their issues. | 1 2 3 4 | Identify their issues and help them formulate ideas. |

6. In a changing environment, I think the creative process works best when it proceeds from:

| Information-sharing, to reflection, to brainstorming. | 1 2 3 4 | Brainstorming, to reflection, to evaluation. |

7. When confronting change, I would:

| Reference previous change experiences. | 1 2 3 4 | Approach the situation from a new perspective. |

8. With regard to the "context" (big picture) and the "goals and tactics" (implementation procedures), when communicating in a changing environment, I would:

| Explain the context—then move on to goals and tactics. | 1 2 3 4 | Set out the goals and tactics—then answer any questions about the context. |

9. In the midst of rapid change, it works best to:

Define a target and allow a strategy to emerge.	1 2 3 4	Formulate a plan and implement it.

10. Because information in a changing environment is subject to continually shifting "knowns" and "unknowns," people often complain that the organization is "telling us one thing one day and something else the next." When communicating in this environment, I would tend to:

Focus on what I know and take questions about the unknowns.	1 2 3 4	Explain fully what I know and what I don't know.

11. When working with people who are struggling in a changing environment, I would focus initially on their:

Feelings and reactions.	1 2 3 4	Tasks and needs.

12. When involved in creative problem-solving it works best to:

Define outcomes, then implement solutions to achieve them.	1 2 3 4	Identify approaches, then try them out and revise them as needed.

13. If I found myself reluctant to complete a task or request, I would first:

Assess the validity of the task or request.   1 2 3 4   Examine the source of my reluctance.

14. When communicating with people in the early stages of the change process, I would take some time, initially, to:

Review the major aspects and demands of the change and ask for ideas and support.   1 2 3 4   Explain the nature of change and the reactions it tends to produce in both organizations and in people.

15. To deal with the increasing demands of change, I would empower teams to:

Independently decide on the best methods to implement specific change goals.   1 2 3 4   Explore and try out different ideas and approaches to help define and address evolving change issues.

16. When communicating to others in a changing environment, I would:

| Share my own feelings about the information. | 1 2 3 4 | Withhold my feelings and focus on issues and ideas. |

17. When a change that clearly represents growth and opportunity is nevertheless causing stress and resistance, I would first want to help people:

| Clarify the benefits of the change for the organization and for themselves. | 1 2 3 4 | Express their reactions and personal concerns about the change. |

18. To keep up with the pace of change, I would first try to identify and isolate current aspects or functions that seem to be changing and:

| Review how we currently handle that aspect and define what we see now. | 1 2 3 4 | Examine the current causes of the change and generate ideas to deal with it. |

SCORING

In addition to an overall score, this assessment will give you individual scores in six key areas:

- **Looking inward.**
- **Creating context.**
- **Setting direction.**
- **Communicating with credibility.**
- **Supporting others.**
- **Generating alternatives.**

To obtain your scores, use the following method. For example, on the sample question on page 25, if you selected option 2 you would *enter the number directly* beneath option 2—in this case, 3—as your score:

If you selected: 1   ② 3   4

Give yourself: 4   ③ 1   0   **Points: _3_**

At this point, refer to your answers and determine your change-readiness scores.

As you'll see below, the highest-scoring response can be option 1, 2, 3, or 4. This variance is the result of our research, which indicates that the most effective response lies on a scale from moderate to high. So, if we found that the most effective response should be practiced strongly, or to a "high" degree, then the highest scoring response will be option 1 or 4. If we found that the most effective response should be practiced to a lesser or "moderate" degree, the highest-scoring response will be option 2 or 3.

1. Looking Inward

Question 2: If you selected: 1   2   3   4
     Give yourself: 0   1   3   4
     Points: _____

Question 7: If you selected: 1   2   3   4
     Give yourself: 3   4   1   0
     Points: _____

Question 13: If you selected: 1   2   3   4
    Give yourself: 0   1   3   4
    Points: _____

Your point total for *looking inward* is: _____

2. Creating Context

Question 4: If you selected: 1   2   3   4
    Give yourself: 0   1   4   3
    Points: _____

Question 8: If you selected: 1   2   3   4
    Give yourself: 4   3   1   0
    Points: _____

Question 14: If you selected: 1   2   3   4
    Give yourself: 0   1   4   3
    Points: _____

Your point total for *creating context* is: _____

3. Setting Direction

Question 3: If you selected: 1   2   3   4
    Give yourself: 3   4   1   0
    Points: _____

Question 9: If you selected: 1   2   3   4
    Give yourself: 4   3   1   0
    Points: _____

Question 15: If you selected: 1   2   3   4
    Give yourself: 0   1   4   3
    Points: _____

Your point total for *setting direction* is: _____

4. Communicating with Credibility

Question 1: If you selected: 1   2   3   4
    Give yourself: 0   1   3   4
    Points: _____

Question 10: If you selected: 1 2 3 4
   Give yourself: 0 1 3 4
   Points: _____

Question 16: If you selected: 1 2 3 4
   Give yourself: 4 3 1 0
   Points: _____

Your point total for *communicating with credibility* is:

_____

5. Supporting Others

Question 5: If you selected: 1 2 3 4
   Give yourself: 4 3 1 0
   Points: _____

Question 11: If you selected: 1 2 3 4
   Give yourself: 4 3 1 0
   Points: _____

Question 17: If you selected: 1 2 3 4
   Give yourself: 0 1 3 4
   Points: _____

Your point total for *supporting others* is: _____

6. Generating Alternatives

Question 6: If you selected: 1 2 3 4
   Give yourself: 4 3 1 0
   Points: _____

Question 12: If you selected: 1 2 3 4
   Give yourself: 0 1 4 3
   Points: _____

Question 18: If you selected: 1 2 3 4
   Give yourself: 3 4 1 0
   Points: _____

Your point total for *generating alternatives* is:_____

Final Score Summary

At this point, transfer your scores to the following summary sheet. You will then be able to see at a glance how you rate—high, medium, or low—in each of the key areas, as well as in overall change readiness.

Summary of Scores

1. **Looking inward:** ____
2. **Creating context:** ____
3. **Setting direction:** ____
4. **Communicating with credibility:** ____
5. **Supporting others:** ____
6. **Generating alternatives :** ____

        Total score: ____

Scoring Key	
Points	
9-12	High
5-8	Med
1-4	Low

72 – 54 High
53 – 37 Medium   **} TOTAL SCORE**
36 – 0 Low

Your scores will show how your responses measure up against what we have found to be the most effective attitudes and practices for leading change. Very likely, you will score high in some areas and medium or low in others. Also, your total score gives you an overall rank of high, medium, or low.

These rankings are broad indicators of potential areas where you are strong and places where you may need to improve. Because they are broad, however, they tend to beg such questions as, "What exactly does 'medium' mean? What should I do? How can I improve?"

As a result, the real value of the inventory lies in examining your responses to individual items and families of items. More to the point, this inventory may have raised more questions than it answered. To further explore and learn about the ideas and issues raised, we invite you now to move into the specifics addressed in this book.

The next six chapters take each of the change-readiness areas in turn. In each chapter, you will receive specific information on one of the inventory items, as well as skills and applications for expanding your knowledge and improving your proficiency.

So, let's get started.

Look Within Before Venturing Out

Look Within Before Venturing Out

We have all heard that self-reflection is a good practice. It's common to find signs on walls and desks that read:

- **Know thyself.**
- **The unexamined life is not worth living.**

But how seriously do we take this advice to engage in self-examination and introspection?

We live in a culture of logic and *action*—one in which self-reflection is often written off as "navel contemplation" or something only for the weak. But is self-reflection really just an esoteric activity for introverted people? Not really. Consider these popular sayings:

- **Get your head on straight.**
- **Look before you leap.**
- **Get your act together.**
- **Survey the landscape.**

All of these everyday phrases express the idea that before taking action, some reflection and observation is useful. So now the idea of knowing thyself doesn't seem so offbeat. Rather, it turns out to be quite normal.

*Reflection doesn't take anything away from decisiveness,
from being a person of action.*
— *Peter Koestenbaum*

Finally, it is important to emphasize that we are not talking about soul-searching or going into a deep state of meditation. However beneficial those activities may be, our focus here is on two areas:

- **Assessing your past experiences with change. What worked and what didn't?**
- **Examining some of your current values, attitudes, and practices. Are they likely to work for you, or possibly against you, in a culture of change and stress?**

DON'T JUST DO SOMETHING, SIT THERE

One of the basic questions leaders should ask themselves is whether it is best to:

Act or reflect?

A strong case can be made for each choice:

Act. In a rapidly changing environment, you need to take action to address the issues you are facing. Do it now! Time is short and it's important to establish some kind of strategy before things get worse. A little observation or sizing up of the situation is okay, but you can't afford to drag out the process. There will always be time to reflect later, to see how you have done, and to possibly make some mid-course corrections. Besides, too much reflection is going to send the wrong message to those who are counting on you for leadership.

Reflect. A changing environment is, by definition, one in which you are operating with less information than you would like to have, reacting rather than responding to events. In short, you are off guard. You want to piece together enough information to formulate some sort of plan. At the same time, you are dealing with the ups and downs of your emotions. You know that mistakes get made when you act hastily or under duress. In this situation, it's best to step back and assess your feelings and plans before rushing into action.

There is merit to both points of view. Each approach also suffers from some false assumptions. The "act" point of view relies on the often-erroneous assumptions that:

- **You know exactly what to do.**
- **You have your emotional act together.**
- **Others may see reflection as a weakness.**

The "reflect" point of view relies on the assumptions that:

- **You need to understand everything.**
- **You have to maintain a positive attitude.**
- **You can't act until you feel ready.**

In this book, we have a bias toward the reflect end of the continuum. We believe that the penchant for action, which has traditionally been seen as the hallmark of effective leadership, needs to be reexamined in the light of change and stress.

Specifically, the value of taking stock—intellectually and emotionally—is nothing less than a survival skill in a turbulent environment. The question is: How can you reflect quickly and in a way that will eventually result in focused and appropriate action?

INVENTORY: MIRROR, MIRROR ON THE WALL

Before getting into more information and ideas, please refer to pages 32–33 and see how you came out in the area of looking inward.

While there are no absolute right or wrong answers here, we have acknowledged our bias toward self-reflection. This bias is based on research and experience that suggests strongly that people who are able to step back and look inward before taking action tend to make better leaders in a changing, stressful environment.

Your rating describes how comfortable you feel in this area—that is, how natural it seems for you to engage in looking within before venturing out.

Here are some sample answers to specific questions that we agree with:

Question 2. Assess the environment—that is, reflect on the facts of the change—before deciding what those facts will mean to you personally.

Too often, people's initial reactions to change are uninformed panic reactions that they then elevate to the level of absolute truth. In other words, people often focus on their own perceptions, reactions, and needs and then make the changing environment conform to these assumptions. Develop a method of looking carefully at the actual facts of the situation before reflecting on what they will mean to you personally. By getting a good grip on what is actually happening, you will be better able to identify the abilities and attitudes that will put you in the best position to deal with the change.

Question 7. When confronting change, draw upon your experiences and revisit what worked and discard what did not.

Because it sometimes feels like everything is changing during stressful times, people often try to come up with a new and improved way of dealing with the situation. They figure old ways of approaching problems will not fit the current circumstances. They are right, but only in part. New situations do call for new approaches. In fact, we've dedicated an entire chapter to coming up with varied perspectives (chapter 6). But one of the strengths of good leaders is their ability to take a hard look at how they've led in the past. What part of their management style and approach was best for communicating with their employees? What tactics tended to result in alienation of the staff? Once you've realized your strengths and weaknesses, you can draw upon these aptitudes to make difficult times as harmonious as possible.

Question 13. When you experience reluctance to complete a certain task or request, recognize your reaction and then reflect on (in other words, examine) your reasons and motives.

When people experience reluctance to act in a changing environment, they often blame the organization or cite external reasons to justify their inaction. In reality, their reaction is the result of their own reluctance to try something new, change their ways, or take a risk. It is very important to take a little time to ask yourself if there is some reason—an experience, an attitude—that is causing your resistance.

For some, looking within seems mysterious or unnatural. When approached in a positive manner, however, it can be quite normal, natural—and useful!

THE CHANGE EXPERT IN YOU

You are already an expert at change, or at least someone with a lot of experience.

To begin your own self-assessment process, it is best to look at how you have handled change in the past. Consider not just whether you *handled* it, but ask yourself how *well*—or poorly—you managed the situation. Be prepared to give yourself some credit, and also be ready to look at what you could do differently. Take a step back and ask yourself:

- **What is the biggest change you have gone through in your life?**
- **What were the circumstances surrounding this change? What caused it?**

- How did you respond?
- What thoughts, feelings, and actions were effective in helping you move through the change?
- What thoughts, feelings, and actions were ineffective and counterproductive; which ones sapped your energy, enthusiasm, or created needless worry?
- What did you learn about yourself during the change process?
- What strengths were revealed that you could now apply to other work or life changes?
- What would you do differently if you were to face this same situation today?

Some people learn from their experience.
Others never recover.
—Anonymous

CAUGHT BETWEEN YOUR STATED GOALS AND REAL GOALS

Oftentimes, but particularly in times of upheaval, people get caught between what they *say* they want and what they *really* want. They get caught between what we call "stated" goals and "real" goals.

Stated goal. A stated goal is what I *say* I want. Stated goals are basically your "to-do" list. They include items like New Year's resolutions, tasks your boss assigns you, good intentions, ideas you read about in books—in general, any *resolve* you make to do something. People are generally aware of their stated goals. If asked to write down ten things you want to get done this week, the only trouble you would have is keeping the list to ten.

Real goals. A real goal is what I *really* want. Real goals are more complex and difficult to define. They are linked to your values, upbringing, habits, and lifestyle. They could include things like not wanting to be rude, a need to succeed, a desire to always treat people with kindness, a distrust of hunches, a penchant for accuracy, or a fear of rejection. Your real goals are so much a part of you—they're so natural—that you aren't always conscious or aware that they are operating.

When your stated goals are consistent with your real goals, you can perform or proceed effortlessly. For example, if someone is told to lead a project that is fairly risky and she has a "nothing ventured, nothing gained" attitude, she won't have any difficulty pushing ahead into uncharted waters. The conscious, stated goal (take risks) is in sync with the real goal or deeply held belief (nothing ventured, nothing gained).

The DuPont Story

But let's consider the case of an executive we worked with at DuPont Corporation. Paul was identified early in his career as a fast-track person. He lived up to his billing and quickly developed a successful track record—a series of "wins" in a variety of areas. Put another way, he had developed a habit of success. So when a marketing crisis hit his area of operations, the first person the organization turned to was Paul.

Basically, his boss told him to take the bull by the horns, try out some new ideas, even if they were risky, and come up with a way to work through the crisis they were facing. Paul enthusiastically took on the "stated goal" of coming up with a new plan. What he didn't realize was that his stated goal of success was about to run into his hidden "real" goal, expressed by his inner belief "I must succeed; I cannot fail."

By asking Paul to "try some things out" (trial and error) and "take some risks," the organization, in effect, told him to fail a little bit in order to succeed in the long run.

The result? He overdid the "safe" elements and avoided or pulled his punches in the risky areas. His idea of trial and error was: all trials must succeed and no errors can exist. And in the end, he failed. His greatest strength became his greatest weakness and, finally, his undoing. His real goal—I am a successful person; therefore I must not fail—ultimately prevented him from taking the kind of bold and potentially risky action that would have allowed him to succeed.

Goals in Sync, Goals in Conflict

Some of the most common "real goals" we have identified that can support or get in the way of your day-to-day stated goals include the desire or preference for:

__Success	__Recognition	__Closure
__Security	__Control	__Peace and quiet
__Respect	__Predictability	__Love
__Order	__Accuracy	__Harmony

Others_____

Look over the list. Check the four that seem to apply to you the most. Feel free to add other real goals that you care about, or that characterize you.

Are real goals good or bad?

Neither.

Real goals just *are*. They are perfectly normal things to want. To seek success and recognition, or harmony and respect, or order and control is perfectly normal—a preference of your personality, the type of person you are.

But could wanting any of these things *too much* get you into trouble?

Absolutely!

When you want, prefer, or would like to get any of these things, they tend to work for you. But if you *have*

to have them, then they work against you. It's the difference between want to and got to—wanna versus gotta.

- **If you wish for success, you will probably be able to keep your actions in balance. But if you *gotta* succeed, you may ride over others and develop a controlling fear of failure.**
- **If you prefer respect and harmonious relationships, you will likely foster good working relationships. But if you *gotta* have respect and harmony, you may avoid confrontation and constantly look for signs of rejection.**
- **If you would like accuracy and control, you will probably operate with thoroughness and accountability. But if you *gotta* have accuracy and control, you will micromanage, over-control, and develop a fear of mistakes and unpredictability.**

Thus, all of your real goals are double-edged swords. They can work for you or against you, depending on whether you are in the *wanna* or *gotta* state. The trick is recognizing which state you are in.

Change, stress, and uncertainty make us all candidates for falling into the gotta state. The effects of change force us up against a wall so that we sometimes react without knowing that we have slipped over the line. And once over that line, those aspects of our personality, style, and value system—the aspects that serve us so well and so positively under less stringent conditions—become emotional and dictatorial taskmasters.

LISTEN TO YOUR BODY

What are your stress reactions? How are you responding to stress and what are you projecting to others?

Everyone has what we like to call a "reaction of choice." This is what happens when someone is faced with stress or change. Some people blow up, while oth-

COMMON STRESS-RELATED REACTIONS		
Physical Signs and Symptoms	**Thoughts and Feelings**	**Behaviors**
Fatigue	Lack of focus	Inability to concentrate
Sleep problems	Nervousness	Overeating
Frequent illness	Irritability	Forgetfulness
Tight neck and shoulders	Impatience	Procrastination
Cold or sweaty hands	Anger	Swearing
Headaches	Depression	Reckless driving
High blood pressure	Helplessness	Oversleeping
Upset stomach	Hostility	Insomnia
Blushing	Loss of confidence	Drinking and drug use
Eyestrain	Frustration	Negativism
Excessive sweating	Inadequacy	Increase in smoking
Constipation/ diarrhea	Annoyance	Belittling others
Nervous tics	Anxiety	
Rashes		
Teeth grinding		

ers clam up; some people get headaches, others can't sleep at night. For many, stress and change cause them to become forgetful or irritable, to overeat or turn away from food altogether. Your reaction feels very normal because you have been practicing it for many years.

You probably already know that one of the most important leadership skills is giving and receiving feedback. Feedback allows you to obtain the information you need to determine where you are, what's going wrong, and what you should and can alter. Fortunately, your body provides you with feedback every day. Under pressure, your body most often responds with three types of stress-related reactions: physical signs and symptoms, thoughts and feelings, and behaviors. Look at the chart on the left. Circle those reactions that make up your "reaction of choice."

Acknowledge Your Control

Let's face it, one of the most common dynamics of change at work is the lack of control you may experience. It's common to feel powerless, normal to feel that you can't do something right away. Unlike these work-related changes and the lack of control you may feel, you do have control over your body and its reactions to stress. Take a look at the list of items you have circled. Now ask yourself: Did anyone else turn on my stomach acidity? Tighten my neck muscles into knots? Force me to eat that second helping of chocolate cake? In stressful times, identifying your body's reaction to stress is a good place to start; recognizing that you can control these reactions is even better. In fact, paying attention to your physical and mental health—eating well, exercising often, breathing deeply, clearing your mind of negative thoughts—has a twofold payoff. You gain more energy to deal with the challenges you face and become more stress-resilient in the process. You also reestablish a semblance of control over your life, control that is sorely missing at this point in your work.

An Inside-Outside View of Stress Reactions

Look back at your list of circled responses. Some of them are internal reactions such as upset stomach or headaches. Many others are external reactions—such as irritability or impatience—which are visible to others. These external reactions affect others, especially those closest to you at work and at home. What is the effect of your reaction on others? Do you know? Can you guess? Will it vary from one person to another?

Your effectiveness as a leader depends to a large extent on how you affect other people. Therefore, knowing how you affect others—the behavior you exhibit, the "vibes" you give off, both positive and negative—is clearly something you have to be able to identify and understand.

Effective change leaders:

- Recognize their effect on others.
- Recognize their particular values and preferences—their "real" goals.
- Monitor their emotional states.
- Repeat the reactions that produce positive effects.
- Reduce the reactions that produce negative effects.

TAKING STOCK

Now that you have examined your history of change, recognized some of your real goals, and identified your typical stress reactions, it's time to take stock.

A little self-reflection is in order. The intent is not to psych yourself out. Rather, we'd like you to recall your experiences and reflect on your reactions and feelings.

As a tool for dealing with change initially and in an ongoing manner, address the following:

1. Givens. The major things I need to accept as "givens" right now are:

_____

_____

_____

_____

2. Strengths. The specific attitudes and behaviors that have served me well are:

_____

_____

_____

_____

3. Checks. Some personal real goals that could potentially get in my way and that I need to check or stop are:

_____

_____

_____

_____

4. Reaction. My "reaction of choice" is:

_____

_____

_____

_____

5. Feedback. Based on the feedback I've received over the years, my effect on people during times of stress and change tends to be:

Positive response:

_____

_____

Negative response:

_____

_____

6. History. Based on how I have handled change in the past, I plan to:

Repeat:

_____

_____

_____

Do differently:

_____

_____

_____

7. **Desired effect.** During times of stress and change, I would like to be:

_____

_____

_____

CONCLUSION

Changing environments call for action. People are looking to their leaders to do something. Thus, an effective change leader is often pictured as a hero on a white horse, a Joan of Arc, who marshals people's efforts, motivates them, and gets things done. This leader may also be seen as someone who likes change—who thrives on chaos—and who is suspicious of people who *don't* feel the same.

Our research and experience suggest that those kinds of heroic change leaders are both unpopular and ineffective. Why? Because they don't realize that the rules of leadership have changed, because *change* has changed. Increasingly, changing environments are being characterized by higher and higher levels of ambiguity and stress. The one-dimensional change hero needs to give way to the multi-dimensional change leader.

In this first chapter, we have suggested that you begin with some simple and straightforward techniques for self-reflection—for looking inward. They are not complex and they don't take long. But the result is that you become more grounded and focused—more *in control.*

A FINAL NOTE ON CONTROL

There is a difference between someone who is "controlling" and someone who is "in control." What visual images do these phrases conjure up?

- **Controlling.** Inwardly focused, uptight, white-knuckled, demanding, and dictating; trying to take charge of a situation by controlling events as well as the thoughts and actions of others.
- **In control.** Outwardly focused, calm, and considerate; observant and attentive; working with people to assess the situation, deal with the stress, and produce a cooperative response.

Looking within before venturing out does not put you in control of the situation—rather, it puts you in control of *yourself* in that situation.

In periods of heightened stress and change, people do not expect their leaders to have all the answers or the ultimate solution. But they *do* respond to leaders who project a sense of control and an outward focus on events and people.

Change leaders should see themselves not as "problem solvers" but as "movement starters."

Context

Clarify
the New
Context

CLARIFY THE NEW CONTEXT

Organizations are pretty good at telling their employees about the details of change—that is, the who, what, why, when, and how of what is happening. Where organizations fail, however, is in their ability to inform people about the new *context* of the change.

So, what is context? Webster's dictionary defines it as follows:

> **con•text** (kän'tekst) *n.* a joining together . . . to weave together . . . the whole situation, background, or environment relevant to a particular event, personality, creation, etc.

Context, then, is basically an interlocking—that is, a joined or woven—set of assumptions that we operate by; the rules we assume to be true in a given situation or environment. As long as the context doesn't change, the rules apply and things work pretty much as we expect them to.

CONTEXT SHIFT—WHEN THE RULES CHANGE

A *context shift* occurs when the rules change; and in the world today we are seeing a number of these shifts. Moreover, these changes tend, more often than not, to take us by surprise. Without warning, we suddenly find ourselves in a situation governed by new rules about which we know seemingly little or nothing.

For example, an organization that has been successfully using direct-mail marketing for years decides to move its advertising online, assuming that the Internet is just an electronic version of direct mail. Suddenly, the organization realizes that web marketing is a different medium altogether—with its own set of rules and assumptions—and learns a painful and costly lesson in context shifting.

Content Versus Context

Before 1980, people talked and complained about change just as we do today, but the changes they were experiencing were largely *within* the existing norms of the time. One might say that the *content* changed but the actual *context* remained largely intact.

Beginning in the early eighties, however, the rules and assumptions we had about businesses and organizations began to fall like dominos. Suddenly, everyone was talking about "paradigm shifts" and developing "new mind-sets." All of a sudden, dealing with context became a central concern for change leadership.

This need to clarify and communicate context has grown unabated ever since, and, with recent events in the world, has shifted into a new gear.

The Reasons for Change

The primary triggers for change, which in turn drive the need to clarify new contexts, are:

58

- Globalization.

- **Technology.**
- **Customer demands.**
- **Competition.**
- **Regulatory issues.**

Organizations create what we call normative states by developing patterns that work. The patterns become standard operating procedure and the context is set. In the 1980s and 1990s, organizations in the areas of telecommunications, banking, healthcare, energy, computers, and manufacturing all had stable operating procedures—procedures that worked.

One by one, however, they were hit with some combination of the following:

- **Deregulation.**
- **Customers wanting things quicker, better, and "their way."**
- **Increased need for, and reliance on, technology.**
- **More competition.**
- **The need to get leaner.**
- **The complexity of the global marketplace.**
- **The demand for new ideas.**

These factors threw organizations into a frenzy. The old patterns no longer worked. Things were falling through the cracks. Systems kept breaking, and then breaking again. Initially, organizations met this revolution with:

- **Denial.** This isn't happening—it'll go away.
- **Resistance.** That's not how we do it around here.
- **Quick fixes.** Let's try this; that should get things back on track.
- **Cuts.** After we downsize, we should be okay.
- **Blame.** If we just get rid of Pat, that will be the end of it.

Organizations tried to catch up, but it didn't work.

. . . there is a Catch-22 to catching up;
*when you get there, "there" isn't **there** anymore.*
— Stanley Davis

WHAT TO DO?

The basic leadership question we are asking is, should I:

Hold the line or embrace the new?

In light of what we have just said, it would appear that the correct response is unequivocally embrace the new. Basically, that's true. But you do need to look briefly at both holding the line and embracing the new in order to get a balanced approach to context.

Hold the line. Obviously, you cannot hold an absolute line—trying to stave off change and keep things exactly the same. But remember, not *everything* is changing. So, while you are dealing with the issues of change, it is important to understand that some things will remain the same, or at least won't change for a while. These include many of your processes, certainly the bulk of your values, and perhaps the cash cow that may go on producing for a while as you move through the change.

Embrace the new. Clearly you need to embrace the new if it hasn't already got you in a bear hug. But what does that mean? Do you know what the "new" really is? Probably not. We can see the symptoms or the effects of the so-called new, but its real identity is vague and still emerging. Trying to embrace it may be like trying to grasp smoke. Something new is coming into being and you have to discern its nature and impact. So let's replace *embrace the new* with *discern the new*.

The idea of not knowing exactly what you are dealing with can be very upsetting to some people. Why? Because they are operating in the old, normative context or mind-set in which things were known and therefore could be handled. Thus, they want the new to be just as clear and manageable.

As a result, your job as a leader is twofold: both to understand and to communicate context. Specifically, you need to:

- **Understand that some basic assumptions and rules of your business or operation are changing.**
- **Accept that recognizing which aspects are changing—and how—will be a slow and often frustrating process.**
- **Avoid the desire or temptation to go for quick fixes.**
- **Learn to rely on your employees—those on the frontline—to help you discern the emerging new realities.**
- **Face the fact that you will, to some degree, be writing a new rulebook on the fly—and that it will probably never be "finished."**
- **Accept continued ambiguity as a normal attribute of your environment.**
- **Communicate to your people all of the above.**

Remember: A new context is frustrating, inefficient, and ambiguous only when you compare it with the old, normative context. In its own right, it is challenging and malleable.

⟲—◆—⟳

Hardy: "Where are we?"
Laurel: "We're right here."

⟲—◆—⟳

INVENTORY: ARE YOU COMFORTABLE WITH CONTEXT?

Before getting into more information and ideas, please refer to page 33 and see how you came out in the area of creating context.

Your score tells you how comfortable you feel in this area—that is, how natural it seems to you to set a new context.

Some of the most effective change leaders regard context in the following manner:

Question 4. Before formulating options or generating plans, take time to examine the implications of any new information coming in about changes.

Organizations tend to rush to generate and implement plans and strategies to deal with pressing change issues. Too often, these approaches are based on incomplete information; people tend to jump to conclusions and don't take the time to assess what's really happening.

Question 8. Start communication about the change by giving an overview of what is changing and why. Then move on to plans and tactics.

Virtually every new communication in a changing environment benefits from giving a short, up-front context or big picture overview. Keep it brief—just enough for people to create a new framework for understanding the tactical information they will be getting.

Question 14. Before asking for their support, involve people—early in the change process—in a discussion of their reactions, issues, and concerns regarding the change.

People want to know what is going on as soon as possible. But, until people feel heard regarding their personal reactions and issues about a change, attempts to explain or promote the change sound insensitive. People may see your comments as your personal agenda, not theirs. As a result, people feel frustrated and undervalued, they tend to withhold their full support, and they take a wait and see attitude. Now let's turn to the skills and techniques for clarifying the new context.

THE FIRST DAY OF THE REST OF OUR LIVES . . . AND BEYOND

Clarifying the new context involves three steps:
- **Read my lips.** Let people know that there *is* a new context.
- **Recognize the old versus the new.** Distinguish between what is changing and what is not.
- **Tease out new rules.** Develop and implement ways to regularly identify emerging issues and needs.

The Context Meeting

It is essential for change leaders to address their people with a clear message about context. The sooner the better. But even if you've been in the throes of change for a while, you still need to have this meeting. Why? Because there is a strong likelihood that people are mentally operating, to some degree, in an old context. As a result, they may be:
- **Wondering when things are going to get back to normal.**
- **Wondering when you're going to tell them what to do.**
- **Doing nothing and waiting for it all to go away.**
- **Engaging in frantic, unfocused action.**
- **Trying to apply old rules to new situations.**

You need to have a meeting or send a message that:
- **Puts a stake in the ground.**
- **Draws a baseline.**
- **Declares that this is the first day of the rest of our lives.**

63

In short, you want to establish a point from which people can mark time. This will be the moment that people will remember as when they achieved consensus about what's going on and attained some clarity on how everyone can work together. Ideally, this meeting will do two things:

1. **Establish a new context.**
2. **Begin the process of defining new rules.**

If you don't have this kind of meeting or experience, your organization will struggle with the new reality. Consider the following story.

The Hotel Story

An executive we worked with at a major hotel chain was in charge of developing new products designed to operate in the same market as timeshares and condos. This effort marked a departure from the organization's normal hotel business. Her people took on the challenge with gusto, assuming that since they were experts in the hospitality business, they should be able to make the transition pretty quickly. They generated ideas, strategies, and plans to get the new enterprise up and running.

The result was a lot of activity, but also a lot of unfocused action, ideas that fell short, and second-guessing. Finally, the executive realized that their inability to make progress was a result of the team not recognizing that they were in a new context—and, more fundamentally—that they were trying to operate under the rules of their old context. As one of her employees put it, "How hard can this be?"

Quoting Dorothy in *The Wizard of Oz*, the executive conducted what she called a "We're not in Kansas anymore" meeting. She went on to clearly lay out the nature of the new market and its implications, specifically noting their lack of direct experience in the condo/time-share market. This presentation fostered a flurry of reactions, concerns, and issues, each of which she noted and addressed, thus legitimizing everyone's opinions. Finally, she held her team's feet to the fire and—comparing the two markets in terms of the team's experience and expertise—made them list what was the same and what was different; what they could keep and what they had to let go of; what they could adapt and what they would have to invent.

This effort was an example of what we call a context meeting—a meeting to get clear in people's minds just exactly where they are, and are not, and then begin to tease out some new rules to operate in this new world with their eyes open.

Remember: In a stable environment, nobody talks about context because the context of that environment is established and known. It's a *given*. It goes without saying. It's like the temperature in a room. When the temperature in a room is ideal, nobody notices or comments on it; nobody says, "Wow, isn't the temperature in here great!" Only when the temperature is too high or too low do people comment.

THE BLOB MODEL

Change is typically characterized as a process of jumping from something old and familiar into something totally new. This perception reflects, more than anything else, the way change *feels*.

For many, change feels like being thrown into a fire or leaping off a cliff into the unknown. This model of change is troublesome because people don't like the idea of being thrown into something totally new.

For others, change fosters a kind of macho "thriving on chaos" mentality (on the surface at least), the notion that you ought to love change and if you don't, then you must be weak. Never mind that you might burn out. Just deal with it.

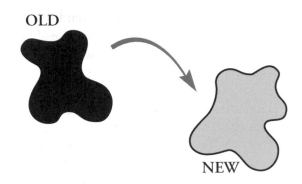

OLD

NEW

Both of these perceptions of change can be hazardous. People can be paralyzed by the fear of change, or burn out from ignoring the changes that are occurring. But more importantly, these conceptions are dangerous because they are not true.

A More Realistic View of Change

One method for helping to communicate the new context to people is through the use of the blob model. In this version of change, the new and the old overlap, creating areas of loss, areas of gain, and a large area that remains the same.

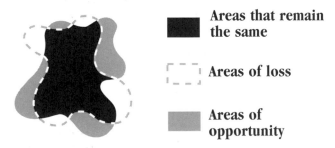

Areas that remain the same

Areas of loss

Areas of opportunity

In the worst case, organizations tend to mourn the losses, ignore the gains, and forget what is staying the same. The result? They obsess about their perceived losses and fail to take advantage of their potential gains.

Best Case

Leaders who deal effectively with change tend to:

- **Acknowledge the losses.** Focus on what is real and what is not; on what is really going away and what is not; then support people in moving through their issues and understanding their feelings.
- **Act on the gains.** Identify what you are getting or dealing with that you haven't seen before. Then distinguish between those "gains" that are troublesome or not worth pursuing and those that are legitimate opportunities for growth.
- **Build on what is not changing.** Remind people that much of the organization and its operational norms will remain intact and will provide the bedrock and the continuity for moving forward.

USING THE BLOB IN A CONTEXT MEETING

To use the blob model as a context-setting piece in a meeting, follow this process:

1. **Present the model.** People tend to like the blob. Let them discuss it for a while. The conversation will start to become more focused as people see the implications of the model not only for understanding but also for dealing with the change. This discussion will lead naturally to the next step.

2. **Make three lists:**
   - Things that are staying the same.
   - Things that will be lost.
   - Things that will be gained.

The list of items that are staying the same will likely be four or five times longer than the list of losses. Focus on clarifying and explicitly defining the losses *and* gains. The more aware people are of exactly what is going away and what has to be dealt with, the less troublesome and more manageable these issues tend to become.

3. Identify "old rules" versus "new rules." Ask people:

- What are some of the old rules, assumptions, and processes that probably won't work anymore that we should get rid of?
- What kinds of new rules, assumptions, and processes do we need to develop to deal with the reality of our new environment—business, technical, interpersonal? The sky's the limit.

This discussion will most likely start vague and get specific. Let people struggle and think. Don't evaluate or judge; simply accept and clarify.

The results of this kind of interaction will be twofold:

1. You will get some good ideas and suggestions.
2. The group or team will feel complimented that someone has given them credit for their ideas and input. They'll also be gratified that the air has been cleared and that they are all now operating off a similar set of assumptions.

Simply *holding* the meeting provides half the benefit. People remember the day that their new roles and rules were defined and use this as a starting point for reinvesting in their work.

CONCLUSION

Taken together, the blob model and context meeting are the means for defining the new reality and operating norms for your organization, department, or team. They are the tools for recognizing that you have to abandon your old context in order to establish a new one, and that the new context will not appear fully formed, but has to be teased out, played with, and defined.

Does this mean that you will be developing new norms as you go along? Yes. Does it mean you will be trying to put together a new rulebook page by page? Yes. Is this process inefficient and prone to mistakes? Yes, but only if you are using normative rules.

In comparison to a stable environment, yes, it is inefficient and often inaccurate. But judged by its own standards, it is the only process that can succeed in an environment in which ambiguity is the norm, trial and error is routine, and mistakes equal learning.

CONTEXT AND SELF-REFLECTION

These first two chapters—"Look Within Before Venturing Out" and "Clarify the New Context"—set the foundation for change management. Our human tendency is to want to race ahead simply because the needs are urgent and the stress is high. But before change leaders can take action, solve problems, and get things done, they must get their heads and their emotions together—as well as help others do the same.

One quick note: Up to this point, we've put the answers to the Leadership Change Inventory within the text of the chapters. Now that you have a sense of how these responses work, you'll find them at the end of each chapter, in gray, next to the Inventory symbol.

So we point you to the skills and tools of self-reflection and context and say—start here! You will then be able to move forward with greater clarity and control.

At first people refuse to believe that a strange new thing can be done,
then they begin to hope that it can be done,
then they see that it can be done—
then it is done
and all the world wonders why it was not done centuries ago.
— Francis Hodgson Burnett

Set a Direction,
Even Though It's Likely to Change

SET A DIRECTION, EVEN THOUGH IT'S LIKELY TO CHANGE

Some of the most contentious areas in a changing environment are the organization's new direction, goals, and plans. People want to know where they're going. They want well-defined goals and objectives. In short, they want clarity and control at a time when clarity and control are, by definition, in short supply. Often, employees' comments include:

- Where are we going? Does anybody know?
- Don't tell me one thing one day and something else the next.
- You're supposed to be in charge. Don't *you* know?

Change leaders often get tied up in these discussions, not because they lack good responses, but because they fall prey to the assumptions of a stable environment in which good leaders *should*:

- Have all the answers.
- Be in charge.
- Set clear directions.
- Develop plans that hold up over time.

As a result, they either get caught up defending the company or avoiding the questions. We have already talked about context, constant change, and high levels of uncertainty. Now it's time to develop an effective method for setting direction and planning.

Plans are worthless; planning is everything.
—*Winston Churchill*

Churchill knew it only too well. He realized that in times of crisis, plans can fall apart as quickly as they are made. Yet planning is still important—in fact he called the process of *making* plans "everything." By going through the process of establishing goals and direction—even if the details of the plans change—you are examining the situation, creating momentum, and inspiring the confidence of your employees.

Direction, especially the plans for heading toward your goals, needs to be flexible in a changing environment. But what does flexibility *really* mean? Often, it refers to the specifics of a plan: Can it be changed and updated? But real flexibility—as we will see—has more to do with your mind-set, with your tolerance for uncertainty and your need for control.

How Can You Set a Direction When Things Are Always Changing?

Change leaders often face the question of whether it is best to:

Formulate a plan or define a target?

Both positions have strong supporting arguments:

Formulate a plan. It is essential that you get a concrete plan in place and begin to follow it. You will certainly have to make mid-course corrections along the way; that's only natural and expected. But if the plan is solid, you can maintain momentum while allowing room for modifications as they come along. In addition, employees have a lot more confidence in a definite plan led by a strong leader.

Define a target. What you need to do is define a target—an outcome. It may change, but probably not too much. Then you can begin to identify some initial steps to take until your actions begin to solidify into something that looks like a plan. That solidification may occur sooner or later; it depends. But you must always be ready for a sudden change or a new idea that you couldn't have anticipated.

In practice, these two methods would probably be very similar. Where they differ is in the mind-set.

The "plan" scenario dangles a very tempting worm to bite. It assumes that your plan is basically good and in need of only "mid-course corrections." It all sounds very safe and logical. But when you bite on that worm, you end up hooked by a plan that is resistant to sudden and unexpected changes and ideas.

The "target" scenario is more open and flexible. It is designed not to get so far in a particular direction that you can't abandon it if necessary. Ideally, it even sets up methods to constantly check and challenge its own validity. The downside of the target scenario is that it is slower to nail things down. This factor can be a real problem for people or organizations with high control needs and low tolerance for uncertainty and ambiguity.

Overall:

- **A plan works forward.** It defines a path and direction, then moves forward to *arrive* at its goal.
- **A target works backward.** It identifies a general outcome, then works *backward* from the goal to bridge the gaps, thus filling in the details of the transition from present to future.

The ideal in a changing environment is to *work backward in order to move forward.* To illustrate this principle, let's examine the pilot and the scout models.

THE PILOT AND THE SCOUT MODELS

The Pilot

A pilot flying from New York City to St. Louis formulates a flight plan, then proceeds to fly the plane to its destination. It's possible, because of weather, for example, for the plane to be temporarily diverted. But most of the time, the pilot flies directly to the destination, making minor mid-course corrections along the way.

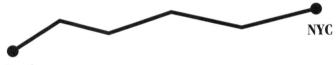

NYC

St. Louis

This system assumes a stationary goal and the accuracy of medium- to long-range planning. In short, it assumes:

- **That St. Louis *is* where we want to go.**
- **That everyone is going to the same place.**
- **That St. Louis will still be there when we get there.**
- **That we have a flight plan to follow.**

The pilot system for defining goals and outcomes is a product of the normative model for organizational development, which assumes that managers and leaders can precisely define the scope and goals for development and therefore make plans that will vary only a few percentage points within a predictable range.

This system further assumes that unpredictability—

the sudden entry into the system of an unknown—is relatively rare and can be treated as an exception to be dealt with on an emergency basis, after which the plan can get back on track.

The IBM Story

An IBM executive once told us that in the early to mid-1980s, "We could pretty much go into a market, determine its strength, project a financial goal, and hit it within 5 percent." As a result, he said, "Our best people tended to be number crunchers."

As the decade wore on, he continued, "all sorts of changes started to come in, the margin of error rose to 20 percent, then to 40 percent, and after that we stopped counting. We found we could no longer predict or plan—and as you know, this hurt us bad . . . and kept on hurting us. We took a big hit in those years."

He contrasted this with their current outlook: "We take a different approach now. We have a whole different kind of person helping us not so much to plan as to set a direction. You need a whole different breed, a whole different mind-set to make it now."

The "different breed" he was talking about can be characterized as the "scout."

The Scout

The scout model takes a different approach. In this scenario, you're going from St. Louis to California in 1850. Although your plan is to head to California, your goal is to find fertile land to farm.

Your wagon train leader intends to follow the California Trail. Yet because he knows things can change, he sends out scouts in advance of the wagons to reconnoiter. If the scout finds that a certain river is too high to ford, that trespassing on certain lands may invite attack, or that there is snow in the pass, he will report back and the wagon train will change its plans.

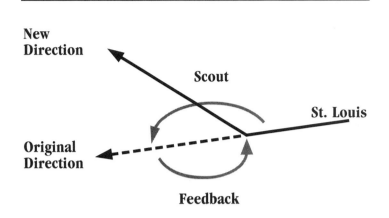

**New
Direction**

Scout

St. Louis

**Original
Direction**

Feedback

Or if the wagon train receives news that there is better land in Oregon, the settlers may even change their
original destination altogether—still fully in accordance
with the larger overall goal of finding fertile land to
settle.

Working Backward to Move Forward

In contrast to an airplane, a covered wagon is a slow,
antiquated means of travel. Yet in comparison to the
flight plan of the pilot, the method used by the wagon
train is a much more sophisticated and flexible means of
planning and execution.

Specifically, the wagon train is *basing its next moves on
regular feedback from its environment.* This does not
mean that the wagon train lacks an outcome and even a
trail to follow. It has both. It has simply developed a
mind-set that is outwardly focused and able to respond
to major or minor changes as a matter of routine.

The primary features of the scout method include:

- A goal or vision that is definite, yet flexible—good
  land to farm.
- An initial plan to get to the destination—a basic
  trail to follow.
- A mind-set that both expects and is prepared to
  respond to change—flexibility in the route.

- A means to get feedback quickly, even daily—via the scout.
- The willingness and ability to respond immediately—to alter course.

In practice, the wagon train is able to *work backward in order to move forward*—that is, use its feedback to regularly update and modify its ongoing plans.

Organizations in the midst of change have to abandon the methods—and, more importantly, the mindset—that make them feel naked if they don't have a clearly defined outcome and a specific means to get to it.

TOOLS OF THE JOURNEY

The whole idea that a map can be drawn in advance of an innovative journey through turbulent times is a fantasy.
— Ralph Stacey

The three key leadership tools for a journey through turbulent times are: defining an outcome; revisiting the outcome while continuously communicating with your staff; and addressing emerging issues.

1. Define an Outcome

Establish a clear and concrete goal or endpoint. People need to know the outcome—what you want to *exist*—when the process is complete.

We are not talking about mission and vision statements here. While steps in the right direction, the mission statements we have seen often lack the specificity and concreteness required by a good outcome.

Let's take a look at an example of a specific, clear outcome. A manufacturing company experienced serious inventory shortages because of a rapid move to diversify its product line. This diversification was in response to sudden customer demand and a competing company's move to capture the same market. The stated outcome was:

> *The right materials in the right place, on time, for the manufacture of models #226 and #228 in black, white, tan, green, and woodgrain.*

It's not very sexy, and it begs for details. But it *is* clear and simple. Exactly how this outcome was to be accomplished was, at first, pretty much anybody's guess. Certainly it had something to do with lean manufacturing principles. The people in the organization had to work out the details, but the target was tangible.

The manufacturing firm's outcome was concrete. But what about the case of a financial organization that just went public? This firm concluded that its processes were fine, but its "culture" was not. An entrenched system of patronage and favoritism had to go. The desired outcome read:

> *Egalitarian management and rewards processes to replace former "old boy" attitudes and practices.*

Sound like code words? You're right—they are. But everyone in the organization knows exactly what those code words mean. It's a more subjective outcome than the manufacturing example—nothing short of a culture shift—but it became much more detailed the closer the firm got to it.

Like the goal of the wagon train pioneers—fertile land to farm—effective outcomes tend to become more specific the closer you get to achieving them.

2. Revisit and Communicate

Regularly clarify the endpoint and the process. A major part of setting a direction that's likely to change is to accept the need for continual updating and revising. The attitudes and practices necessary are:

- **Release yourself from the responsibility of having to have "the plan" up front.**

- Accept that the outcome may change or evolve.
- Expect that the tactical plans will change and evolve almost daily.
- Establish a forum or process to check progress and to define new plans on an as-needed basis.
- Get closest to the people who are closest to the action, those who can provide you with information about customer needs and market demands.

A journey requires continual attention and revising. As a result, change leaders need to implement and enforce a new process that makes it normal to meet frequently to informally discuss and alter plans.

3. Address Emerging Issues

Expect and respond to the unexpected. To expect the unexpected is almost a contradiction in terms; and certainly, to have plans in place for every contingency is impossible. What *is* possible, however, is to monitor the environment in a proactive way in order to identify and address emerging issues, rather than get blindsided by them when they hit full-force.

In chapter 6, "Remember, There's Always One More Way to Look at a Situation," we will present a tool for identifying emerging issues. Until then, suffice it to say that any situation in flux is by definition prone to unexpected, anomalous factors that seem to come from nowhere. Dealing with emerging issues can be made much easier by developing a mind-set to expect them and a process to recognize them.

CONCLUSION

What the world needs *least* is a new process for setting goals and objectives.

For almost three generations, we have been inundated with methods like MBO (Management by Objectives) for gaining the upper hand over our environments. These processes were popular less for their success than for their promise of predictability—that we, by employing these methods, could achieve *control*.

Unfortunately, these methods assumed that we always knew what our outcomes actually were.

Management by Objectives works if you know the objectives;
90 percent of the time you don't.
— Peter Drucker

In his book *Managing the Unknowable,* Ralph Stacey observes that the dominant mind-set among many leaders today is that they "must find the right kind of map before they launch their businesses upon the perilous journey into the future." This approach, he adds, is a result of our "scientific education . . . countless management textbooks and development programs."

What is needed instead is a different attitude and some simple rules of thumb to address a changing environment on its own terms. These rules of thumb include:

- **Focus outwardly.** Focus on the environment, not your plan.
- **Revisit frequently.** Frequently update your outcome and revise your plans.
- **Expect surprises.** Establish a means to detect and respond to surprises.
- **Work backward.** Establish clear outcomes; work backward to determine what you need to accomplish them; then fill in the gaps.

Never tell people how to do things. Tell them what to do,
and they will surprise you with their ingenuity.
— George S. Patton

Inventory: Plans and Directions

Now that you know a little more about planning in a changing environment, let's review the inventory items addressing that issue.

Your rating for setting direction describes how comfortable you are with ambiguity and uncertainty, and how natural it feels to allow plans to develop at their own pace without an initial fixed plan to guide them.

While there are no absolute right or wrong answers in this area, our research and experience strongly suggest that establishing clear and evolving outcomes at the beginning of the change process, and then allowing plans to develop and clarify as the process unfolds, is the most effective approach to "planning" in a changing and stressful environment.

The best leaders are relatively flexible. Here are some strong sample answers to the specific assessment questions on setting a direction:

Question 3. Instead of defining specific plans and tactics, it is more effective—not to mention more realistic—to supply people with outcomes and goals that are clear, but also flexible, in other words, subject to change as conditions develop.

Ideas in a changing environment are designed to address perceived problems and issues. As the change develops, however, your perception of these issues and problems will undoubtedly evolve. Therefore, instead of putting a lot of effort into formulating specific goals and objectives early in the process, it is better to identify broader outcomes as clearly as possible, but with the expectation that they may evolve and change the closer you get to solving them.

Question 9. Define general outcomes or "targets" when addressing new issues; then allow your plans to emerge, evolve, and solidify as you proceed.

Because of the nature of change, you cannot just set plans and follow them. Plans tend to become outmoded very quickly. Rather, you need to establish an outcome or target and head toward it, allowing the specifics of your tactics to gradually solidify and emerge. As a result, you will work backward from your outcome to continually update and revise your plans. Your job as a change leader will be to help people deal with the uncertainty and the perceived lack of control as the final plan is clarifying itself.

Question 15. Empower teams and groups not just to implement defined goals, but to allow for the problem to change; explore and try out new options and approaches.

Often, teams are charged with managing their own efforts in the implementation of known solutions. Ideally, in a changing environment, teams do not assume the existence of clear and unchanging goals and outcomes. Rather, they assume that because the outcomes are still evolving, they will need to keep exploring and redefining the issues they are addressing, allowing ideas and plans to evolve and work themselves out. Change leaders need to continually communicate and have faith in their teams to reach the best outcome.

COMMUNICATE WITH CREDIBILITY

Credibility is an important element of every leadership encounter, but it becomes even more important in times of change. At the most basic level, if you are not credible to your people, they won't believe what you say and they won't trust what you do. Time and energy that could go into productive work instead get sidetracked by negative thoughts and conversations in which you play the main role. In the worst-case scenario, people you depend upon may leave, disengage, or even actively sabotage the company's efforts if they don't find you trustworthy and credible. But what is credibility? Why is it so important in times of crisis? Is it something that can be built?

Credibility is others' perception that you as a leader are trustworthy and real. It is the measuring stick that people use to determine if there is congruence between your words and deeds. The formula for gaining credibility looks like this: $C = T+O+V$.

In which:

C = Credibility

T = Trust

O = Openness

V = Validity

Want to have a greater level of credibility? *Easy.*
Enhance your trust, openness, and validity. Easy to say,
that is. Let's take a closer look at each element.

Trust

While fostering trust is always important, it takes on
greater significance when the environment becomes
unpredictable. In a stable environment, trust is more of
a one-dimensional item and has largely to do with this
question: Does the leader follow through on what he or
she promises?

The changing environment, by definition, is unpredictable. In other words, it can't be trusted. The leader
may also be deemed untrustworthy when he or she says
one thing one day and something else the next. So then
people ask: Whom or what can I trust here?

Notice that the question no longer has to do simply
with promises and follow-through. There is now an element of the unknown, along with an emotional dimen-
sion—including worry and anxiety—that was not present before. While people may ask for assurances, what
they really want is someone to trust.

Openness

Studies show that people who disclose information—
and get others to share—are perceived as trustworthy.
Openness allows communication to proceed in two
directions. It gives permission for people to approach
you not only with feelings, but also with the information and suggestions that you need to become a more
effective leader.

A key element of being open is the ability and willingness to self-disclose. But many things can get in the
way. Disclosure may run counter to your personality,
you may be more of an introvert, or the workplace culture may not support this practice. You may also struggle with knowing what to say and when to say it.

We'd like to assuage your fears and point out something that we've seen over and over again, namely, that moving in the direction of disclosure—even taking a few baby steps—goes a long way toward helping people trust you.

Validity

Math and science are disciplines based on logic. For an analytical person, an argument, in the logical sense, is not a conflict involving feelings, it is an exercise in objectively trying to establish a relationship between cause and effect. When this link is established without contradiction, the argument is valid. We say of a valid argument, "if its premises are true, its conclusion must be true."

Under normal circumstances, most people evaluate the work environment and its leaders primarily using what is known as face validity. In other words, your employees will most likely examine things at a superficial level, just paying attention to the surface and how things appear to them. They may cut you a lot of slack and inherently trust your intentions and plans. As we mentioned in the introduction, in times of heightened stress, people often become hypervigilant. In this state, they no longer are content with a superficial view of the situation, they look more closely at the "premises"—the conditions, stipulations, and particulars of the situation—and this involves looking much more closely at you.

What are they looking for? They are trying to find what we call disconnects, the inconsistencies in what they believe you are thinking, what you are saying, and what you are doing. They examine the premises under a microscope and if they find that they are untrue . . . so too must the conclusion be false. Without validity, without congruence of thoughts, words, and action, credibility goes out the window.

As you read about the three ingredients of credibility, you probably noticed that they are more than additive, they are synergistic. Openness and disclosure build trust. Trust is a requirement for validity. Validity and congruence promote openness. This interrelationship is demonstrated in the model that follows.

THE THREE CONVERSATIONS MODEL

To better understand how the trust-openness-validity dynamic works, let's take a look at the three conversations model.

The First Conversation

ME ⟷ **YOU**

In this conversation, ME is you, and YOU is someone else—a colleague, a boss, an employee, a friend, or a spouse. Your lives are basically a series of ME-YOU conversations.

The Second Conversation

While you're having this first conversation, you're also having a second conversation—with yourself—called the ME-ME conversation (also sometimes called an inner dialogue).

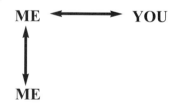

Suppose you are having a ME-YOU conversation in which you are trying to be positive or reassuring, but in the conversation with yourself, you are saying things like:

- I'm worried about this change.
- It will never work.
- I don't know what I'm doing.
- I wish I weren't here.

Question: If you are saying these things to yourself, does the other person know it?

Answer: Yes!

Your contradicting conversations create a disconnect. The other person does not know the exact content of your ME-ME conversation, but the tone of your voice, your body language, and your eyes all signal that what you're saying and what you're feeling are different. As a result, the other person's self-talk—the YOU-YOU conversation (his or her own inner dialogue)—may be something like this:

- I'm hearing one thing but sensing another.
- I don't know where I stand.
- I don't know if I can trust this person.
- I wish I weren't here.

The result of this disconnect is a false or wooden conversation at the ME-YOU level. You are being positive on the surface, but the real conversation is taking place in undertones of misunderstanding and mistrust.

**Actual conversation in
tones of mistrust**

The other person does not believe you, but more importantly, this person will probably feel that you cannot be trusted.

So, how do you remedy this situation? One way is to make your ME-ME conversation positive. But what if you really do have negative feelings or concerns? Here's where openness and self-disclosure come in.

The Third Conversation: Openness

The best way to address this situation is to develop what psychologists call agreement or correspondence; in short, to make the ME-ME and the ME-YOU conversations *agree*. This is the third, and most effective, version of communication in the three conversations model.

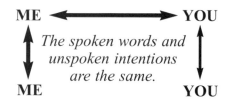

You need to bring the thoughts and feelings of your ME-ME conversation into the ME-YOU conversation. Express your reservations as well as things you feel confident about; share some of your own thoughts and feelings; tell people what you know and what you don't know; be straight with them. In short, strive to make sure that what you are saying is supported by what you are thinking and feeling.

When other people are asked to describe people who demonstrate this level of agreement or correspondence—that is, self-disclosure—they most commonly use words such as *open*, *trustworthy*, and *readable*, as in, "I can *read* him."

Thus, the three conversations model provides us with an almost clinical description of the elusive concept of *trust*. We can say with authority that self-disclosure equals trust; that openness fosters credibility and buy-in.

All of which leads us to our key question: Should I encourage myself and others to:

Hold back or open up?

The traditional arguments for these two choices are:

Hold back. In a business or organizational environment—particularly one characterized by change—it is best to stay away from expressing emotions. The problems in the environment alone present enough conflict as it is, and emotions only add unwanted baggage to the task of solving the problems at hand. More to the point, emotions tend to obscure the real issues and can unnecessarily upset you and cloud your thinking. Therefore, you should remain as dispassionate and businesslike as possible.

Open up. In times of change and stress, people have reactions, thoughts, and concerns. In short, they have feelings. The combination of their thoughts and feelings creates a total reaction that is very real and therefore deserves to be addressed. Emotions do not obscure the issue; rather they help define its scope and importance. Only when people feel understood can they emotionally free themselves up to think about solutions and next steps. Therefore, to help them open up, you should open yourself up a little more.

We could make a case that to allow people to open up is the best strategy to foster trust in a changing environment. The three conversations model certainly supports this point of view. Or better, we could argue that if you prevent people from opening up, not only will you drive their frustrations underground, you won't be able to hear the real issues they are facing.

But, like so many things . . . *it depends.*

It depends on:
- How comfortable you are with expressing feelings.
- How much you plan to disclose.

- The needs of the other person.
- How comfortable *they* are with expressing feelings.

Here's how one executive worked through these concerns.

The Chemical Bank Story

Just before it merged with Chase Manhattan Bank, Chemical Bank underwent a number of wrenching changes in its operations area. We worked with one executive who had the unenviable task of telling his people a number of things they didn't want to hear. Basically, he had to say, some of you *might* lose your jobs, some of you *will* lose your jobs, and many of you will be working in a new area. And in the meantime, we need your support to make it through this transition.

"Yeah, right," he said. "They're not going to believe a thing I say, and they're going to hate me." As a result, he decided to get it over with quickly; tell them the basics and hope for the best. "Less is more," he reasoned. "And whatever you do," he told himself, "don't tell them what you really feel, it will only make them more upset."

In effect, he had decided to limit the amount of information people would get and deny them the chance to read his ME-ME conversation.

"That's a good strategy if you want to crash and burn," we told him. "But if you really want to get their commitment to move through this change, you've got to tell them everything, especially what you don't know, and also let them know how you feel about it all."

"Why would I do that?" he asked incredulously. "They'll just resent me more."

"Whether they like you or not is not the point," we told him. "What they need is to trust you—specifically, to trust that you are being perfectly straight with them and that you have their best interests at heart as they move through a difficult time."

"Let me get this straight," he asked. "You're telling me I'm going to foster trust by letting them know what I *don't* know and how I *feel* about it?"

"Basically, yes," we responded.

The strategy worked, and here's why.

TELL 'EM WHERE YOU'RE COMING FROM

As a change leader, you continually find yourself in the position of having to give people assignments, communicate information, and answer questions. In other words, you have a series of ME-YOU conversations. Some are formal; most are not.

Because of time pressures and the number of these interactions, there is a tendency to make them as brief and efficient as possible. In terms of the three conversations model, you are giving them the bare bones of the ME-YOU conversation (all external dialogue) and denying them your ME-ME conversation (your inner thoughts). This is a recipe for distrust and discomfort. To add to the problem, you may also be denying them the explanations of your information, thus limiting their grasp of the overall context.

Therefore, to foster credibility and buy-in, you'll need to cover the following:

- The "what." Specifically what you know and what you don't know.
- The "why." The rationale, big picture; that is, the context.
- Disclosure. How you feel about what you're communicating.

Let's take them one at a time.

The "What"

The "what" is simply the content or the information you need to share. You will always provide this information, of course, but it is important to say what you know as well as what you don't know. Why? Simply because, unlike a stable environment in which there is a lot of information and few unknowns, changing environments are characterized by sparse or insufficient information and many unknowns.

Not wanting to look stupid, some change leaders avoid what they don't know and end up with communications full of gaps and holes. This leads to two negative outcomes: People think you are withholding information, and they have an opportunity to fill in the information vacuum with rumors and misinformation.

"But if I tell people what I don't know," one executive lamented, "they'll think I don't know what I'm talking about."

"Not to worry," we told her, "they already know you don't know what you're talking about. But as long as you pretend you do, they won't trust you or support you."

Disclosing what you don't know is a form of openness. It sends a message that you have the courage in yourself and the faith in them to speak the truth and therefore foster an environment in which you can both work to fill in the blanks and address the issues.

The "Why"

In addition to the details, people want to know the "why"—that is, the rationale, the big picture—in short, the *context*. We have talked at length about context in previous chapters, but suffice it to say that no matter what the issue, it is a good idea to ground or contextualize the information you are giving. Perhaps more than anything else, it is a courtesy to the person and fosters a greater degree of openness and trust in you as a leader.

Disclosure

Far and away the single most effective part of your communication is your ability to self-disclose.

When asked what they want from their leaders—specifically in their communications—people begin with the basics: what, how, why, who, when, and what's in it for me. But they always add something like: "It would be nice to know how he feels about this" or "where she's coming from on that."

When asked why it would be important to know the leader's thoughts and feelings, people commonly tell us:

- I could trust her more.
- I could get into his head.
- I'd know where we stood.
- I'd know if he really believed it.
- I'd know how to gauge the situation better.

These subjective responses express an intuitive sense we all have, namely, that when people disclose something about themselves others tend to trust and believe them more and feel more personally in control.

But how do you do it? What does disclosure look like, sound like? Here are some guidelines for the most appropriate ways to share your feelings.

Signal the shift

Get the information out on the table and then, before going on to something else, signal the shift to self-disclosure. For example:

- Before I get into the details, let me tell you where I'm coming from on this.
- I'm excited about this—I wish we'd done it a year ago. Let me explain why.
- If I were you, I probably wouldn't like this idea at first.
- I need to be frank with you here.
- Now there are parts of this strategy that keep me up at night.
- I'm not unmindful of the hardship this is going to work on many of you.

- **I think we are all feeling some mixed emotions here.**

These simple phrases signal to the people you're talking to: "Listen up! Here comes the ME-ME." Then they sense that they can trust you.

Keep it short

Disclosure should be brief and focused on your thoughts and feelings, your reactions, or your take on the situation. A little goes a long way.

Also, you don't necessarily have to be good at sharing your feelings in order for disclosure to be effective. If you are uncomfortable with expressing emotions, don't worry. People will see that you are trying and will probably credit you even more for gutting it out. In other words, you can get an A for effort. Remember, it's not what you say as much as it is that you say it. They are reading your intent, not your content. Your meaning can be clear whether you're polished and comfortable or not.

Don't overdo it

Self-disclosure is not gut spilling, it is not maudlin appeals, it is not your opportunity to share all your pain and suffering. Your task is simply and honestly to share your thoughts and feelings about what you are communicating. Speak honestly and clearly and let the ME-ME / ME-YOU dynamic do the rest.

Self-disclosure is nothing more than affording people some information with which they can read you. If they find you trustworthy and credible, that trust will transfer to the information you are presenting.

In an environment filled with uncertainty, changing information, and stress, addressing these dimensions is essential for a complete communication. It is a technique that fosters trust and mutual openness, as well as encourages openness in others. Put another way, it gives them permission to have the very feelings that they are already having.

Validity Is in the Eye of the Beholder

So far in this chapter we've spent time focusing on you, specifically how you get your message across. Now it's time to turn our attention to the recipient of your communication. Here's where it helps to remember that "validity is in the eye of the beholder."

Just as good leaders know that they must tailor recognition and rewards to the unique needs of the recipient—some people value public praise, others written thanks, certificates, or time spent with you—so too do effective leaders tailor their communication to the individual. The goal is to deliver a message that the recipient deems meaningful and valid, a message that is directed toward his or her specific personality type.

The concept of personality types and innate preferences was advanced by the pioneering Swiss psychologist Carl Jung in the early twentieth century. Jung described a number of types—groups of individuals who shared a natural tendency to perceive the world and interpret information in a common manner. Jung's work forms the basis for a number of popular style-based assessments, the most well-known being the Myers-Briggs Type Inventory. The PowerSource Profile is another Jungian-based assessment, but one that can be applied to worksite groups in a time-efficient manner. It also has the advantage of being specifically tailored to individuals' stress and change patterns.

The profile identifies four specific types:

- **Creative people.** A preference for imagination and intuition, a forward sense of time, and a tendency to become stressed because of fragmentation, lack of attention to detail, and difficulty with follow-through.

- **Grounding people.** A preference to use the senses, be practical and realistic, favor tried-and-true procedures and rules, and be stressed by changes to the predictable and orderly.
- **Logic people.** A preference for cause and effect, objective analysis, model building, and quantification; stressed by having to make decisions without enough data, and by situations (and people) with strong feelings.
- **Relationship people.** A preference to interpret information based upon how it will make others feel, keen attention to their own emotions; stressors include having to say "no," getting burned out, and taking criticism personally.

In order to tailor your communication to different types of people, you need to abandon a "one size fits all" mentality and open your eyes and ears through observation and inquiry. Ask yourself: Am I dealing with a high-creative, high-grounding, high-logic, or high-relationship individual? It is true that all employees need some of the same things at the same time. They all have a need for information, to know what is going on. They need to have their feelings acknowledged and validated. They need to understand the new structure and to recognize where they fit in. And they need to have a vision of the new organization. But the different energy types differ in the degree to which they require these things. Specifically:

Creative people: While creative people are often good at instigating change, they also react to changes thrust upon them. Creative types tend to be the most confused individuals, those who scurry around the most. When their creative energy runs amok, they visualize worst-case scenarios (particularly those people who are high in both creative and relationship). One of the best ways to relate with them is to "walk and talk." Encourage them to take a stroll with you. The rhythm of exercise often has a calming effect and promotes a more orderly flow of information. Highly creative individuals are quick to see new possibilities. What they need to envision is how their unique abilities to come up with new possibilities and ways of working will be used and valued in the new structure. You can help by painting this type of picture for them.

Grounding people: They are most upset by the change in structure and the loss of predictability. They fear the new order of things. Grounded people tend to be among the most resistant to change and are the slowest to give up attachment to "the way it was." They may express anger at their loss of identity and for the change itself. They respond best to a very focused, step-by-step discussion of the situation. Praise their ability to see things through. Help them identify *one* tangible benefit of the change. Provide them with a reason to develop new roles and skills and an orderly approach for doing so. Keep your illustrations and examples concrete. Avoid the temptation to overwhelm them with information.

Logic people: According to their processing system, the change may not make sense. They think it is not smart, that the organization is embarking on the wrong path, making the wrong decision. They argue about the best direction to have taken. They no longer have a clear model for themselves. High-logic people will regain their comfort when they have well-defined, quantified organizational goals and a model of what the new system is going to look like. Let high-logic individuals know that you value their analytical and decision-making skills and that the organization will need to draw upon these abilities more than ever. Sketch out a picture or model of the new structure, the corporate objectives, and add whatever measurements seem appropriate. Go over the timeline for any changes and get their input into the sequencing of activities.

Relationship people: In changing times, they take on additional emotional burdens, having concerns not only for themselves but also for coworkers and family members. They miss the camaraderie, the intimacy, and sharing they had with their teammates who were laid off. The environment constantly reminds them of their departed colleagues. They are prone to spend time reminiscing, for example, "When Joe was here, he used to laugh like that." You have to let them talk it out, all the while legitimizing and validating their feelings. Attend to them with good eye contact and encouraging body language. Let them know that you have heard what they have said and that you value them for their concern and caring. It takes time to help relationship-energy people work things out until they feel good again.

Moving Ahead

The guidelines above can be helpful in moving people away from the old and toward the new reality. Focused, tailored communication goes a long way in satisfying the intellectual and emotional needs of the audience. This combination of elements, moreover, has the ultimate effect of creating a mutually shared bond of confidence between you and your people.

CONCLUSION

All of us are investors. Some big. Some small. When it comes to investing our money, the first question we ask is: Can I trust this financial adviser, company, and market with my investment? Just as important is the investment that employees make not only with their bodies, but with their hearts, minds, and spirits. Do they trust us enough to fully invest in our organization? Do our words, feelings, and actions match?

You'll find the phrase "get it together" many places in this book. It represents the value of congruence, which is best exemplified by one of our favorite stories:

In the late forties, Indian pacifist Mahatma Gandhi presented his country's desires for independence to the British Parliament. Gandhi was so eloquent and passionate that members of the audience wondered how he could present without notes, charts, and other oratory devices. His press secretary responded that it was simple. "What Gandhi thinks, says, and does are one. You think one thing. You say a second. You do a third. That's why you need notes to keep track."

One of the best ways to build or maintain trust with your people is to make sure that what you think, do, and say are one—even if you are simply saying "I don't know." Your employees will find you more credible and they'll be more likely to reinvest their efforts in the organization.

Inventory: Do You Communicate with Credibility?

Openness creates validity, and validity fosters trust and credibility. Our experience suggests strongly that people who demonstrate and foster openness tend to make better leaders in a changing, stressful environment.

You rated yourself in terms of how comfortable or how natural it seems to you to engage in disclosing your feelings and sharing the whole story.

The best change leaders approach communication as follows:

Question 1. Say what you feel—strive to make your statements about specific aspects of the change consistent with your feelings about those aspects.

Putting on a positive face or in some way hiding your real feelings from others is not a good strategy in a changing environment. Not only does this practice prevent the open discussion of issues, it also gets in the way of cooperation. People who say one thing but are thinking or feeling something else are almost always betrayed by their body language and their tone of voice. As a result, they are viewed as closed and hard to read—and ultimately untrustworthy.

Question 10. Account for all information regarding the change—both what you know as well as what you don't know.

Leaders often avoid the subjects about which they are unsure or do not have complete answers. In other words, they avoid addressing topics that they are uncertain about because they don't want to appear out of the loop or ambiguous. This is a self-defeating practice. As a leader, you need to account for both what you know and what you don't know. If you avoid the unknowns, you will create holes in the communication. As a result, people may accuse you of hiding information—or even lying—and will certainly fill the holes with rumors and negative information.

Question 16. Practice self-disclosure; when communicating, share your own opinions and feelings about the information you are discussing.

Telling people how you feel about the information you are communicating—in other words "where you're coming from" or "what keeps you up at night"—may be the single most important factor in the communication process. You don't need to overdo it; a little goes a long way. People who risk disclosure are perceived to be honest and credible. In short, people tend to believe and trust them. In addition, leaders who disclose their own reactions and feelings model the behavior and communicate that it is okay for others to express their emotions as well.

Take the LEAP with Your People

Take the **LEAP** with Your People

By far the most common—and urgent—question we hear from leaders in a changing environment is: "Do you have anything to help me help my people?" Other comments include:

- They're coming to me and I don't know what to tell them.
- I've got the same issues and concerns myself.
- I tell them one thing, it changes and then they blame me!
- They're bouncing off the walls; my boss says, "Fix 'em." I say, "Are you nuts? You need Sigmund Freud to fix them."

Have Your Feelings at Home?

The job of a leader is to lead, and to lead means working with people and their needs. In a changing environment, these needs are often urgent, strident, and raw. In the face of this challenge, some leaders buckle—like the change leader who told his people, "Look! If you want to have feelings, have them at home. This is a business."

Nice try, but it won't work. Whether you like it or not, whether you feel like you signed on for it or not, dealing with people—their needs, upsets, and issues—that's your job! And you don't have to be a psychologist to do it. You do, however, have to understand people's resistance to change.

When dealing with people, remember you are not dealing with creatures of logic, but with creatures of emotion.
—Dale Carnegie

CHANGE AND HUMAN RESISTANCE

Most people easily recognize the obvious and overt forms of resistance—anger, objections, arguments, and challenges—and generally respond to them to one degree or another.

There are many more subtle forms of resistance, however, which are ignored, pushed aside, or not even noticed. These include:

- **Confusion.**
- **Concern.**
- **Misunderstanding.**
- **Disagreement.**
- **Distrust.**
- **The need for proof.**
- **The need for control.**
- **Worry.**

You will be able to see or sense resistance—provided, of course, you are focusing outwardly, or paying as much attention to the other person's reactions and questions as you are to your own agenda. Specifically you need to:

Be aware. Be ready to pick up the body language, changes in tone of voice and facial expressions, as well as the overt statements that signal resistance.

Stop and shift. Be prepared to temporarily give up your agenda and respond to the person's resistance. Most interactions will present a number of these shifts.

Let Go of False Assumptions

As soon as you are ready to jump in and address resistance in others, however, another spectre arises—the spectre of your own potential false assumptions. These often "heroic" assumptions include:

- **I need to have all the answers.**
- **My job is to make people feel good.**
- **I am in charge.**
- **I have to put on a confident face.**
- **I have to solve people's problems.**

These attitudes come from the normative, stable environment's definition of what a leader is. This command-and-control mind-set tells leaders: You're the boss. You need to know everything. You shouldn't show any cracks in your confidence. You're responsible for how people feel. You're in charge.

Maybe we have exaggerated this mind-set a bit, but you get the point.

We have already addressed some of these assumptions. By being more open, by telling people what you know and don't know, by helping people jointly define their own context, and by examining your own attitudes and feelings and disclosing them, you have hopefully changed some of these assumptions and gained some skills for leading in times of change and uncertainty.

This set of tools concerns the need to help people express their feelings and identify some options in order to address their issues and concerns. Notice that we didn't say "fix" their problems or make them "feel good." The operative words are "express feelings" and "address issues."

But where do I start the process of dealing with resistance? Should I:

Focus on feelings or focus on issues?

Here are the arguments:

Focus on issues. It's the issues, not the feelings, that are important here, so the sooner you strip away the emotions and get down to the root cause and identify some actions, the better. Otherwise, you're just sitting around listening to bellyaching and doing a lot of hand-holding. People ought to be adult enough to put aside their feelings and get down to working on specific cases.

Focus on feelings. People need to know that their leaders really understand "where they're coming from" emotionally so that they can be free to take action. If this doesn't happen, they'll feel that nobody is listening to them—or cares! All the problem-solving in the world won't be effective without this understanding.

We have phrased both of these arguments in the extreme to make the point that neither answer by itself is going to work. Put another way, the approach here is not "it depends," but rather "yes, both." It's simply a matter of sequence. Which do you do first?

Answer: focus on feelings—then focus on issues.

People Need to Be Heard

This point is one that most people already know intuitively, namely, that before people can get down to solving problems or taking advice, they want to be sure that the other person really *understands* what they're saying.

This entails listening and acknowledging both the content and the emotions of people's statements. If you cut a person off too soon, if you jump to a solution before they've finished venting a little, their sense is that you don't want to get mixed up in their problem, that you don't understand or don't care. As a result, your "help" comes off as false, uninformed, or maybe even your way of getting them out of your hair.

In short, the key is *Empathy*—with a capital E. The so-called "soft skill" of empathy is not soft at all. It has a steel core running through it. It is an observable, measurable behavior which, when coupled with a problem-solving component, is nothing short of the single most effective survival skill in a changing environment. One manager discovered the power of empathy by mistake.

The Mayo Clinic Story

An executive hospital manager at the Mayo Clinic told us about the experiences that he had when the clinic was in a protracted period of change. People were coming to him almost hourly with questions, complaints, and concerns, as well as warnings, ultimatums, and threats. Because he was the type of person who wanted to remain positive and make people feel good and not worry, he embarked on a conscientious program of optimism, assurances, and solutions.

"How's it working for you?" we asked.

He just rolled his eyes.

Then one day, one of his people, complaining about getting blindsided with a last-minute assignment, let loose with a burst of anger, finally blurting out " . . . and as a result, I missed my little girl's dance recital!"

The manager was so affected that, almost speechless, all he could say was, "That's *terrible!*"

"You're darn right it is!" the woman replied, at which point she became "strangely satisfied," as the manager put it. "From that point forward," he added, "we were able to calmly discuss and address the issue." He later reinforced the principle that when people are upset, they don't want answers or "fixes," they just want to be *heard*. He noted with irony, "It took a situation that was so bad that I couldn't think of anything to say but 'That's terrible!' to teach me that."

113

We rest our case. What the manager realized is a simple truth, one that we all know intuitively, particularly if we've been on the receiving end of someone trying to make us "feel good."

When you empathize, you do not necessarily "fix" things, make people feel good, or resolve all the issues. As the manager told us, "We still had plenty of issues, and we still don't agree on everything, but we *are* able to understand each other and talk." Empathy—the validation of one's emotions—is the doorway to trust and respect and the beginning of problem-solving.

How Empathy Works

The R in the illustration below represents resistance. When you meet resistance, your natural tendency is to want to overcome or resolve it by moving the other person toward what we call "+1," the positive.

At +1, you tend to respond with statements such as: Don't worry. We can handle that. Have you thought of . . . That's not so bad. You think *you* have problems!

In short, you marginalize people's resistance and pain with pat answers, assurances, and solutions. You tell them, in effect, "Don't have your feelings, have *my* feelings. Mine are better."

Your intentions are generally positive. You want to make people feel better, assure them that their issue is not serious, or convince them that their concern should not be a concern—all in the name of helping them. You feel that the sheer weight of your experience and background and data will be enough to reduce their fears and comfort them.

But what is it like to be on the receiving end of all of these well-meant comments? The effect is for the person to be knocked back to what we call "–1," the negative.

At -1, the person tends to hear: My feelings aren't valid. My concern is silly. You're too busy to deal with my questions. Why don't you ask an intelligent question? Yeah, yeah, yeah . . . Shut up and sit down.

Thus, the total dynamic is as follows:

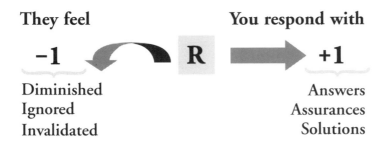

They feel	You respond with
−1 R → **+1**	
Diminished	Answers
Ignored	Assurances
Invalidated	Solutions

Question: So how do you address this problem?

Answer: You need to first legitimize the person's issue or concern and only then help them move to address it. In short, you need to empathize and help the person LEAP.

THE LEAP PROCESS

LEAP is a mnemonic device whose letters stand for the steps of effective communication. These include your ability to:

- Listen.
- Empathize.
- Ask.
- Propose.

Let's take a closer look at each.

Listen

To listen well, you need something to listen to. People's first statement concerning their issue is often just the tip of the iceberg. In order to surface their deeper concerns, ask the magic questions: Can you tell me more about that? What do you mean? Can you explain?

Now the person is talking. As people talk, however, you will probably feel the impulse to counter, argue, reassure, prove wrong, yes-but, or set straight. As they are talking, therefore, a switch should go off—the switch labeled *shut up!*

Then train yourself to keep quiet for a moment. *Don't talk; rather, listen.*

By resisting the temptation to talk, you gain three very valuable tools:

- **Time.** You buy time to collect your thoughts and emotions.
- **Information.** You discover the identity and details of the issue.
- **Credibility.** You allow people to express themselves and feel heard.

The other person is talking; you are listening with both your eyes and your ears. You are thinking and focusing; the person is clarifying and letting off emotions which, if you were to argue, would be directed at you. But when you listen, the emotions are not being directed at you as much as they are simply being *expressed.* In the L stage, just listen and nonverbally respond.

Tell yourself: "I don't have to defend, argue, assure, fix, summarize, explain, cajole, or justify. I just need to listen."

116

Empathize

After you have listened, your temptation will be to jump to the ask and propose stages—the problem-solving parts of the process. At this point a second switch needs to go off—another important switch—*empathize*. This stage is clearly *the most crucial stage of the process.* If you do it well, the relationship and the process will pick up and move on. If you don't, it won't. It is fair to say that at its core the LEAP process is a delivery mechanism for empathy.

Empathy means simply to:
1. Understand how someone else feels.
2. *Demonstrate* that you understand.

The key behaviors to provide empathy can be expressed in the words *acknowledge* and *legitimize*.

To acknowledge is to say something that lets the person know that you understand his or her feelings, such as "I see your point," or "I'd feel the same way," or even something as brief as "Wow," or "I hear you," or "Fair enough." Even a nod or raised eyebrow can do the trick.

The key here is to acknowledge; that is, to communicate to people that they get to decide how they feel.

Even seemingly stereotypical statements such as "I hear you" or the infamous "I feel your pain" can be effective. The key is not in the words, but in your intent, usually carried nonverbally or in the tone of your voice.

There are three general categories of empathy:

1. **Identification.** You identify or agree with the person's feelings.
   - I think I can understand how you feel.
   - You're absolutely right to react that way.
   - I can totally identify with that.
2. **Observation.** You want to let the person know that you recognize the emotion and its intensity.

- So, you feel that was uncalled for, right?
- You're really mad!
- I can see you're upset.

3. Justification. You acknowledge that their reaction is valid given the events.

- I'd feel the same way if I were you.
- I can see why you reacted the way you did.
- Anybody would feel that way.

As you can see, empathy is not necessarily sympathy. You can legitimize another person's reactions and feelings without having to agree with them. In fact, agreement or disagreement is not the point here. The other person is going to feel the way he or she feels whether you agree or not. In most cases, people really don't care if you agree.

The emotional dynamic at play here can be described as one of release. At the core, people simply want someone to know how they feel—preferably you, but a bartender will do. Having got it out, and having someone else legitimize it, provides an emotional release. The person, in effect, exclaims, "Finally! Someone knows how I feel!" Once this release is accomplished, the person can move on to see the issue more objectively and begin to generate options and ideas.

At this point, you shift to the A and P stages—ask and propose. These are the problem-solving parts of the process, when it is appropriate for your "fix it" tendencies to kick in.

Most managers and leaders are already pretty good at these skills, but we need to review the basics.

Ask

To ask is to gather information necessary to begin addressing the issue. Specifically you need to:

- **Gather information.** Make sure that you have all the facts and the context surrounding the issue.

- **Summarize.** Repeat the basics back to the person to ensure that you got it right.

Depending on the situation, the asking stage may take a long time, or it may be very brief. Be thorough, but don't overdo it, and when all the necessary information is on the table, move on to the propose stage.

Propose

Notice, your job is to *propose*, not present.

What's the difference? The word *present* has an air of formality to it as in, "Okay, here's the plan." Fait accompli. You are better served by the word *propose*, which has an air of tentativeness and cooperation to it, as in, "Here's what I propose. Tell me what you think. Work with me."

The propose stage may result in drawing up a plan, but is more likely to result in identifying some next steps. The results of the propose stage ideally will include ideas for mutual action, that is, some combination of what you have to do and what the other person has to do. In short, you want to:

- **Identify your next steps.** Define simple but specific actions for one or both of you to take.
- **Identify an outcome.** Define what you want to exist once the actions have been taken.
- **Arrange a checkpoint.** Set up a time to get back together or to communicate how things are going.

People have hopes and ideas. They also have feelings—and these feelings often pop up and get in the way of our rational and "business-like" dealings. When they do, they can disrupt and derail the learning process and the working relationship. You ignore feelings at your peril. But you can address them by using LEAP.

CONCLUSION

The key skill of leadership is leading—that is, leading *people*. These people have ideas, thoughts, and questions; but they also have concerns, reactions, and feelings. An effective leader must be able to address people's intellectual issues and their emotional concerns. More to the point, the most direct path *to* the issues is *through* the emotions. Understanding and legitimizing people's reactions and emotions buys you the trust and credibility—and the permission—to address their problems.

In this chapter we have given a special status to empathy. While nobody disagrees that empathy is a good thing, some are puzzled by the importance we give it. In twenty years of dealing with change management and developing materials to help people deal with change, we have seen a steady growth in the importance of this skill.

Why is Empathy So Important?

In a stable environment, people can rely to a large degree on the security of the system. As a result, they feel more in control and can move easily from circumstances to problem-solving.

In a turbulent environment, the system is shaky. It can no longer meet people's needs and solve their problems.

At these times, people turn to each other and to their leaders. They want to be heard, they want to find out if anybody else feels the way they do, they want to know that other people are dealing with and expressing *their* issues and feelings—that it's okay to do that—and they want to know that the leaders will offer a combination of clarity, congruence, and compassion to help them work through their own issues

Empathy is not mere soothing or pity. It is a powerful tool for leading change.

Inventory: How Do You Provide Support?

Now that you have had a chance to learn about the importance of the LEAP process, let's see how you responded on the inventory. This will help you review the key points of the chapter.

Our research and experience strongly suggest that allowing people to be heard and then legitimizing or validating their feelings is a key skill, if not *the* key skill, in an environment of stress and change.

You rated yourself in terms of how comfortable you felt in this area—that is, how natural it seems for you to empathize before delving into other issues. Specifically:

Question 5. Legitimize other people's feelings; that is, summarize and accept their feelings and reactions as normal and appropriate to the situation.

People want confirmation that what they are feeling is valid; that it is normal to feel the way they do under the circumstances. Thus, the secret ingredient of change management is empathy. Sometimes, people just want you to listen and nod your head. Other times, an observation like "I'd probably feel that way too" or "You're really angry" can be very effective— and is certainly much more helpful than saying "Don't feel that way" or "Here's what I think you ought to do." At that point, people really don't care what you think; they just want you to listen and not dismiss their feelings.

Question 11. Help people who are struggling with change to clarify their reactions and feelings before moving on to ideas and solutions.

People who are struggling generally want to be heard—they want someone to know exactly how they feel. If you try to engage them in problem-solving before they have had a chance to express their concerns and issues, you send the message that you don't care about their concerns or don't want to bother. But once you listen and help them clarify their issues—once the emotional hurdle has been cleared—people feel unburdened. They are able to see their issues, and possible solutions, more clearly.

Question 17. Hold off discussions regarding the benefits of the change until people have had a chance to express their reactions and personal concerns.

Organizations often rush to promote the benefits of their strategies in order to make people feel good or to sell the change. This tactic often backfires because people get the impression that the organization doesn't care and doesn't want to know how they feel. People are going to have questions and reactions no matter what the change, and allowing them to express and clarify these issues buys you trust and credibility as a leader.

Remember,
There's Always
One More
Way to Look at
a Situation

REMEMBER, THERE'S ALWAYS ONE MORE WAY TO LOOK AT A SITUATION

One of the greatest demands of changing environments is the need for new ideas. And one of the most ignored activities in this environment is taking time for actually *generating* new ideas.

Why? Because when people are in the throes of organizational chaos they barely have time to put out all the fires they are fighting, much less generate new ideas. As a result, organizations move in fits and starts, blindly trying to come up with new approaches to emerging problems.

The traditional tool for fostering creativity and developing new ideas is brainstorming. Everybody knows the rules for these sessions:

- **Identify a problem.**
- **Throw out ideas. Anything goes.**
- **Don't edit or evaluate.**
- **Go for quantity, not quality.**

The purpose of this session is to capture multiple ideas or solutions to a problem. Most brainstorming sessions conclude with evaluation. They whittle down the list of possibilities to one or more probable approaches to a problem. In general, these meetings last from one to two hours; the sessions *do* generate ideas, and people generally feel pretty good about the solution—giving it an average score of 8 on a 10-point scale.

What's interesting, however, is that when those same people are asked to reevaluate the same idea three days later, they give it an average score of 3 to 4. What happened in the ensuing three days? Well, whatever it was, it's an indication that something's not working right.

But does the difficulty lie with the idea they generated or with the process by which they achieved it?

We're going to make a case that the difficulty is with the process. Specifically, we contend that the traditional brainstorming session—which is supposed to harness the creative process—works against the way your brain likes to operate and generate ideas.

BRAIN FRIENDLY

We assert that the traditional brainstorming process is brain *un*friendly.

So, what is brain friendly? Or put another way, how do brains prefer to operate? What's the brain's idea of a good time? What are the best conditions for brains to generate new ideas?

We can approach the question of how to generate alternatives by asking should I:

Generate ideas, then act on them, or reflect on a problem, then generate ideas?

We'll hear what the brain has to say on this matter in a moment, but first let's examine arguments for each position.

Generate ideas, then act. Once the problem or issue is defined, it is important to brainstorm solutions and allow people to begin acting on these ideas. With the right combination of people, you will come up with a number of good and actionable options. Time is crucial in the change process. If you use some of that valuable time to brainstorm, you had better not let the effort die for lack of attention.

Reflect, then generate ideas. Once you and your team have defined the problem, it is best to set aside a short period of time to go away to think about it—to sleep on it. After people have had a chance to process the information, bring them back together to share their ideas and options.

The traditional organizational response for generating ideas is, as we have mentioned, brainstorming. In a changing environment, this sort of session becomes even more important because of the pressure to get results. Thus, the agenda reads: meet, brainstorm, evaluate, implement. We believe it should read: meet, share information, go away and reflect for a while, return and generate ideas.

To explain why this approach works better, consider the following exercise.

OUT OF THE BLUE

We have all had the experience of getting an idea seemingly out of nowhere, or, as it's often described, an idea out of the blue.

Below is a question relating to such spontaneous ideas. As soon as you read it, an answer will immediately pop into your mind—probably two or three answers. When they hit, write them down or remember them. Are you ready? Regarding these ideas that suddenly come to you:

Exactly *where* and *when* do you get them?

Don't turn the page until you answer the question.

Do you find that ideas often come to you in some of the following places:

- A car, or something to do with driving?
- In bed, either out of a dead sleep or just before you wake up?
- In the bathroom—showering, shaving, brushing teeth, etc?

When we conduct this exercise with groups, these are almost always the first three areas that are mentioned. We then push the group to give us all the times and places that ideas come to them. A common final list looks like this:

Car/driving	Reading	Daydreaming
At a bar or restaurant	Dozing	In a meeting
Listening to music	Airplane	Housework
Doing yard work	Sleeping	Place of worship
Listening to the radio	Showering	Watching TV
Playing with kids	Shaving	Exercising
Talking to someone	Ironing	Thinking

Then we ask: "What's missing from our list?"

Answer: Work!

With the exception of "in a meeting" or "talking to someone," work-related problem-solving sessions seldom make the list—and then only as one of the last items. Brainstorming almost never appears.

Let's look a little more closely at these ideas.

What are these ideas about?

Basically anything. The ideas you get are always in response to something you have been concerned about, something you've been thinking about, or something that's been bugging you. It could be personal or business—but whatever it is, it's important to you.

Do the ideas really come out of nowhere—from out of the blue?

No. You have had them for a while. It is only because of their suddenness and often their clarity—and the fact that they come at times when you are not consciously thinking about them—that they seem to come from nowhere.

How can people get these ideas if they haven't been thinking about them?

Actually, they *have* been thinking about them. Interestingly, a problem, concern, or question goes into the human brain in the same way that a "solve" command goes into a computer. From that point onward, the subconscious works on the issue until it comes up with an answer or a response.

Why do ideas come during downtime such as in the shower or while driving?

When you are actively thinking about something— whether it's a work-related dilemma or something else altogether—you are engaged in conscious thought. Think of it as being on the phone with yourself; you are having a conversation with your conscious mind, trying to solve a problem. In the meantime, your subconscious is working on other issues. Moreover, your subconscious is better at creative problem-solving than your conscious mind because a very large part of the brain—what author and neurologist Dr. Richard Restak characterizes as the *association cortex*—is "devoted to establishing networks and thereby linking everything together throughout the brain."

Eventually this part of the brain comes up with an answer or an idea and immediately wants to call you up on the phone and tell you. But it can't. Why? *Because the phone's busy!*

⤝⬦⥰

> *Whenever I think, I make a mistake.*
> — *Roger Stevens*

⤝⬦⥰

Only when you hang up—that is, stop monopolizing the circuit—can the call from the association cortex get through. And when do you hang up? When you are driving, showering, sleeping, listening, etc.

Most of these activities can be categorized as basic motor skills (driving, exercising) or routine mental skills (listening, reading). Other times when your brain is receptive to new ideas include sleeping and altered states such as drinking or meditating. But whatever the category, your brain is on automatic during these periods. You can drive or shower without thinking; you can think faster than people can speak or faster than you can read.

So, when you hang up—*Zap!* The idea comes through, suddenly, often fully formed and seemingly out of nowhere.

Incidentally, when you are in a brainstorming session, who are you talking to on the phone, the conscious mind or the association cortex? Answer: the conscious mind—the line is busy and the most creative part of your brain can't get through. Traditional brainstorming sessions are generally brain unfriendly.

Finally, there is nothing mysterious about the brain's creative problem-solving process. You are actually very familiar with it at an intuitive level. It's the process people rely on when they say, "If I just stop thinking about it, it'll come to me. It always does."

---

*All the really good ideas I ever had came
to me while I was milking a cow.*
— Grant Wood

How Your Brain Works

We have just presented you with some facts about your brain and how it processes information. Now you know a little more about the brain's idea of a good time. Basically, your brain problem solves in the following manner:

- Your problems and issues go into your brain like a "solve" command goes into a computer.
- When you click an icon on a computer, the computer is off and running; even if you call up other functions, the computer is still working on that initial task. In the same manner, once entered, the brain will work on your problem until it comes up with a solution.
- Depending on the issue, it normally takes a little while for the brain to process the information and come up with an answer. The brain generally does not like to be rushed or pressured.
- The solution or idea the brain comes up with is only as good as the information it has available.
- The message from the association cortex can only get through to you once you "hang up" on the conscious part of the brain.

Given all this data, what can we conclude regarding generating ideas in general, and identifying options in particular? The most valuable conclusion is simple and obvious: Instead of having a one- or two-hour brainstorming session on Monday, it would be better to:

- Hold a 45-minute to one-hour session on Monday to define the problem and share information.
- Allow people to go away for a while and process the information.
- Meet on Wednesday or Thursday for 45 minutes to an hour to share the ideas that people have come up with.

The Ad Agency Story

One manager we worked with at a major advertising agency has the brain-friendly process down to a science. We were discussing an issue in her office when she stopped suddenly and said, "Maybe we need to scan this one." Without explaining what "scan" meant, she picked up the phone and told her assistant, "We need to have a scanning meeting. Fifteen minutes."

In 15 minutes, seven people showed up in the conference room. The manager outlined the issue and the group, without any prompting, spent about 20 minutes listing facts and asking questions. The manager, who had been taking notes, read back a quick summary of their contributions, whereupon they all got up and left.

"What was all that about?" we asked.

"We have an agreement around here," the manager explained, "a deal you might say, that if someone has an issue they want input on, they can call a scanning meeting. Anybody who is in the office is honor bound, as we like to say, to meet for 20 to 30 minutes to scan the issue, that is to give input and ask questions to broaden the scope of the issue."

"Then what?" we asked.

"We let it sit for a while, then meet again and see if anybody has any additional insights or ideas," she replied.

"Why don't you ask for ideas right away—in the first meeting?" we inquired.

"We find that we get better ideas if we wait a few days."

This manager and her department discovered on their own the basics of the brain-friendly process of defining an issue, creating an interval of time to think, and reconnecting to share ideas. Better yet, they incorporated this into a kind of organizational habit, a routine practice with a big payoff.

THE THREE DS

We call this process "The Three Ds":
- Data dump.
- Downtime.
- Draw out.

Adopting this simple procedure has two very important benefits. It honors:

1. **The organization's need to generate ideas as quickly as possible—in effect, to put creativity on a schedule.**
2. **The brain's preferred method of processing information and solving problems—thus making the process brain friendly.**

1. Data Dump

A data dump is the essential first step in an effective creative process. We mentioned earlier that the alternatives and ideas that the brain generates are only as good as the information it receives. If the information is poor, then you have the situation, in computer terms, of "garbage in, garbage out." But if you can bring a number of people together to share their information, then the likelihood of an effective solution or idea increases.

The purpose of the data dump is to provide a forum for dispersing and sharing information. Although the data dump follows the basic rules of brainstorming, it is not brainstorming per se. The purpose of the data dump is not to come up with ideas. Ideas will come later in the draw-out session. Rather, its purpose is to "dump the data"; that is, to share all the information available on a given issue or problem.

Brain mapping

The most effective method for dumping the data is brain mapping (or mind mapping). There are a number of very good books on this subject, but the basics are as follows:

133

- Define the issue or problem to be addressed.
- Reduce this issue to a word or phrase—for example, "inventory" or "eroding values"—and write the phrase in the middle of a large sheet of paper or on a whiteboard.
- Using markers or Post-it notes, allow a short time (4 to 5 minutes) for people to write or post anything and everything that has to do with the issue.
- Observe the rules of brainstorming—anything goes.
- Next, allow another 4- to 5-minute period for people to connect one or more of the items on the board with a line and briefly address why these elements are related.
- Allow time for people to explain why they connected what they did.
- End the session and set up a draw-out meeting for two or three days later.

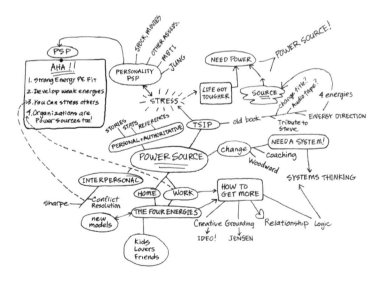

Mind map created during the writing of PowerSource *by Dr. Mark Tager and Stephen Willard.*

This method is brain friendly and brain effective for the following reasons.

There's no pressure

Unlike the traditional brainstorming exercise, there is no expectation that this initial data dump must come up with an idea or solution. No pressure. As a result, the brain is free to absorb and begin to assimilate the information. If you do get an idea in this session, no problem. Write it down and bring it to the draw-out session. The main function of this meeting, however, is to share as much data as possible so that whatever ideas and approaches you ultimately come up with will be based on a rich reserve of information and connections.

It's information rich

The main theme of this session is: Two heads are better that one; five heads are better than two. The more participants the better—up to about 12 or so. The process strives to pull out as much information as possible from many different sources and points of view. The part of the process in which people connect items and explain their connections serves to jumpstart the brain's association process.

There are numerous modalities

It has also been shown that the quality of the eventual output is enhanced by the number of modalities—visual, auditory, and kinesthetic—that are involved. Simply put, the combination of talking, writing, drawing, posting notes, discussing, observing, and using color gives the brain more variety and more things to associate—and as a result, a better final output.

2. Downtime

Once the data dump is over, allow time for the participants to go away—to their showers, cars, beds, or wherever—and let the information simmer. Two to three days is optimal.

It is also important that people get in the habit of recording the ideas they get during this time away, lest they forget them. We stress this practice because when the brain makes a connection—gets that idea out of the blue—it secretes a powerful dopamine, causing a pleasurable "aha!" or "Eureka!" feeling. This reaction creates the sensation, as one person put it, that "I would never, ever—never!—forget the idea." But as soon as the dopamine fades, so too does the idea. So, use a notepad or a tape recorder to catch these ideas before you lose them.

3. Draw Out

Two or three days later, assemble the same group of people to share and explain the ideas or suggestions they came up with during their time away. Since these ideas will probably be in a variety of stages of completion—from specific suggestions to hunches—it's best to allow people to log in, that is, to present their ideas without interruption or discussion. Then, with the ideas and themes on the table, help the group discuss and analyze and then select the best idea or combinations of ideas.

Like brainstorming, ideas produced by these sessions get an average score of 8 on a 10-point scale. But, unlike the products of the brainstorming session, they still get the same score of 8 three days later.

EMERGING ISSUES

The data-dump, down-time, draw-out process is designed to capture the best of the brain's preferred method for solving problems. There is also a shorter process for capturing what we call emerging issues. Try the following exercise.

Emerging Issues

Select an aspect or function of your work that seems to be changing, then complete the following:

1. In the past, we accomplished this aspect by . . .
2. We did it that way because . . .
3. Lately, however, I've noticed . . .
4. Which leads me to think or wonder if . . .
5. And, as a result, I think we might want to . . .

Did you have any difficulty completing these sentences? Probably not. Most people find this exercise easy to finish—and surprisingly useful! Typically, your answer to number 5 will fit into one of two categories:

1. A specific idea or approach.
2. A more focused definition of the problem or issue.

With either type of answer, the exercise has proved useful. We call this process one of identifying emerging issues because it is most useful in getting a handle on issues and situations that are just beginning to show themselves. Often we sense their presence by their effects, such as having too much of this or not enough of that; or observing that the same questions or issues are repeating themselves.

In response to these new issues, organizations in change tend, in effect, to stick a finger in your face and demand:

- What's causing this? I want answers!
- What's the problem here? Deal with it!
- What are your emerging issues . . . huh? . . . huh?

These pointed demands try to jump you from the symptom to the solution in one step. The brain doesn't like that sort of pressure and will most likely respond with what it thinks you want to hear, or with nothing. But by allowing a few minutes, dropping back a little and taking a running start at the issue, people find that they can come up with some valid and valuable ideas and options.

The secret of our exercise is in the sentences themselves. First, the brain cannot help but complete an unfinished sentence. Brains appear to put great effort

137

into finishing the unfinished and creating a whole from parts. Think of the "What's wrong with this picture?" cartoons in the newspaper.

Second, the sentences themselves reflect the familiar. They ask you to simply observe, that is, to comment on what you've noticed, and then ask for a conclusion. In this manner, you are able to move from the past to the present to the possible.

We have found this template very effective for individuals, but particularly for groups, to get an initial sense of what might be some of the new or emerging issues in their areas or departments. Two practices seem to work best:

1. **Give all participants the same issue, let them complete the sentences, then compare notes and discuss.**
2. **Allow people to select their own issues, complete the sentences, then compare notes and discuss.**

The result of such an exercise is that, in a short time, you will identify one or more ideas or an approach to one or more important issues. From these issues and approaches you can begin to formulate the "new rules" of the changing environment that we discussed in the context chapter

CONCLUSION

In this chapter we have addressed the need for generating alternative ideas and approaches in a rapidly changing environment. Also, we've had a little fun with phrases like "what do brains like to do" and "the brain's idea of a good time." But our point is a serious one, namely, that understanding how the brain works and how it processes information gives us simple and powerful options and possibilities.

Specifically, the skills and tools presented in this chapter—the *data-dump, downtime, draw-out* process and the *emerging issues* template—are designed to capitalize on the optimal abilities of the best problem-solving tool you've got—your brain.

There will be some who object to this idea of demystifying creativity and the notion that our brains all work in basically the same way. They would argue that the creative process is ultimately individual and ineffable. Their sentiments bring to mind one of our favorite statements.

*The brain is an amazing and wonderful instrument—
able to transform a vast amount of information,
creatively and uniquely, into an infinite and
unpredictable array of sublime thoughts and ideas.
But of course, this is the brain's opinion.*

The brain is predictable. Or to put it another way, it can be counted on. Like the computer analogy we mentioned earlier, feeding problems and issues into the brain or presenting it with unfinished sentences is indeed like clicking an icon on a computer screen. And once clicked, you set in motion a neurological process that will work literally day and night to address your issues, come up with options, and present them to you—if only you will allow yourself enough time and opportunity to pay attention to them.

Inventory: How Do You Generate Alternatives?

Our research and experience suggest that in an effort to meet immediate demands for quick solutions, organizations tend to either ignore the creative process altogether or try to push it beyond its limits and end up with ideas that, in the long run, do not prove effective.

Your rating describes how comfortable you are with the practices and attitudes that we have found to be the most effective for generating solutions and approaches in a rapidly changing environment.

The strongest change leaders approach creativity in the following manner:

Question 6. Supply all participants with the same information, then allow them some time for reflection before analyzing and identifying new approaches.

Before idea generation can be effective, it is necessary to clarify the issue as you see it and then generate a common body of information about that issue with your people. Brain-mapping techniques are effective at this stage—followed by a two- to three-day interval during which people tend to spontaneously generate ideas and approaches. At that point, you can draw on the new ideas people have come up with. These more well-thought-out ideas often prove to be much more valuable to the organization.

Question 12. Instead of trying to brainstorm, develop, and implement final solutions for emerging issues in a changing environment, it

is more effective to test out new ideas on a trial basis, then use that feedback to refine and inform the next steps.

Organizations facing changes often put too much time and effort into brainstorming in the hope that they will quickly come up with the right solution. It is more effective to accept that creative problem-solving is an iterative process, one in which it is best to test out ideas in a rough draft or "half-baked" form and then use that information to learn about and improve your approach.

Question 18. Identify and isolate specific areas or aspects of the organization that appear to be changing and see if they are part of a pattern.

Organizations experiencing change tend to instigate sweeping programs to bring operations quickly into line. These quick fixes assume that the organization has isolated the cause of the problem. What often happens is that the decision makers end up 1) changing things that don't need to be changed, 2) ignoring key issues that should be addressed, and 3) missing possible patterns or trends. It is more effective to observe and clarify the symptoms—the indicators that tell you something has changed or isn't working—and then develop and try out options to address those issues.

KEEP BALANCE IN MIND

So far, we've examined six skills that can help you when working with your people. In this seventh skill, we're going to shift focus slightly and address the question: How good are you at staying balanced during stressful times? While the primary focus is on you, these skills can also be directed toward others. In many ways, managing yourself is a testing ground for managing others. Many of the balance skills you will use to become more personally centered and effective can also be shared with your peers and subordinates at work. And, as you may already know, a healthy, balanced leader is a better leader.

An Image of Balance

Work today is a series of sprints. Technology has increased expectations and shortened deadlines. People want information, reports, samples, and products now . . . and at lower prices. To stay competitive, many companies are scaling back their staff through mergers and downsizing while at the same time attempting to get to market even quicker with new products. In a realm where they're asked to do more with less, many leaders tell us that balance may not be possible. To which we ask: Is there anything you can do to give yourself more energy to handle the challenges of work? If, for periods of time, you are involved in sprints that cause you to feel unbalanced in the short term, do you also keep the big picture in mind? If you're unbalanced in the course of a day or a week, are there ways to make sure that the whole month has better overall balance?

When asked to come up with an image that represents balance, most people envision the scales of justice, a tightrope walker, or a seesaw. Some people picture a circus performer juggling balls in the air. What these images have in common is that each is *dynamic*. The moments of stasis are rare; they are objects in motion with the laws of physics at play. Force, mass, and acceleration are at work. Subtle movements can cause big results.

Achieving balance is a juggling act, made particularly difficult by the often-conflicting demands of work and life. Before we go on to discuss the skills in this chapter, we'd like you to explore the following exercise. On the illustration on the facing page, take a moment to label the issues, in other words, the "balls" you are dealing with at work and in life. Once you've finished your drawing, step back and ask yourself:

- How do you feel about the number and type of balls you are juggling? Too many, not enough, just the right amount?
- Which are the balls that get dropped as pressure mounts?
- How important or unimportant are the dropped items?
- Are you the only one who can handle each of these demands?

The trick to juggling is determining which balls are made of rubber and which ones are made of glass.
— Unknown

Write your demands and
issues of work and life in
the spaces provided. Add
other balls as you see fit.

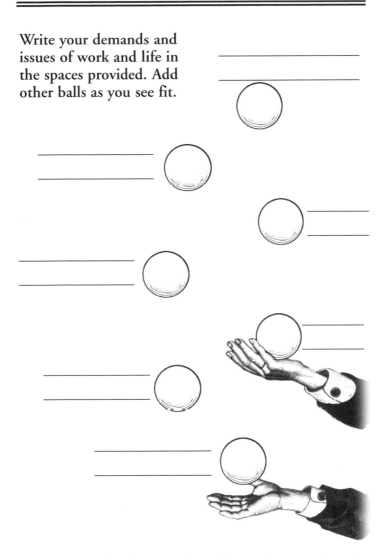

Most people who complete this exercise note that the balls that get dropped most frequently deal with things such as eating well, exercising, relaxing, and spending quality time with family members and friends.

Yet, as a business leader, you have work to do. In order to be successful, you have to attend to the emotional needs not only of yourself but also of your people.

So the question to ask is should you:

Focus on work or engage in life?

The arguments for each point of view are:

Focus on work. Now is the time when you have to rise to the occasion, to buckle down and get things done. Your organization needs your time and attention more than ever before. There's a lot riding on your performance. Plus, your people need you to take the LEAP with them. You'll have time for yourself later.

Engage in life. There's more to life than just work. Is a life without reflection and family worth it? In ten years, will any of this matter? After all, you're no good to anyone if you don't have your health. If you get sick you can't do your job, so you need to take care of yourself. Besides, when you start burning out, you make poor decisions that can cost the company time and money.

Given the popularity of work/life programs and renewed attention to quality of workplace culture, there is a tendency to think that "engage in life" is the correct response. The challenge of achieving balance is that both answers are right, but neither is complete without the other. This may seem paradoxical. Can you focus on work and engage in life simultaneously if there's only so much time in a day, week, and month? To have it both ways is not easy. There are, however, skills that can increase the likelihood of balancing your personal life and work. Using these skills appropriately means first learning about the economy.

MACROECONOMICS REDEFINED

How much is a country worth? It depends. The balance sheet of the United States, including equities, real estate, pension funds, credit, and other financial assets, is about $50 trillion. But according to University of Chicago professor Gary Becker, this figure is only a fraction—some 20 percent—of the total worth of the U.S.

if one includes *human capital*. Human capital represents what people bring to work—their knowledge, skills, health, and values. Examine any company's finances and the human contribution far outweighs the value of physical assets, yet it never appears on any financial reports.

In personal health management, value is also not expressed in dollars, but in units of energy that are available for productive thoughts, meaningful feelings, and appropriate actions. Just as you can accumulate wealth by reducing the drain on capital and increasing the supply, the same formula applies to personal well-being. Let's take a closer look at the two sides of the capital/energy equation:

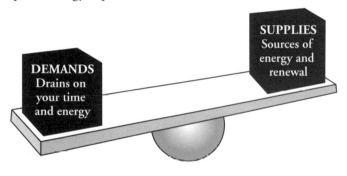

DEMANDS ON YOUR ENERGY

Most people are pretty good at identifying how, when, and where energy mismanagement occurs. They can identify situations and people that rob them of their vitality and focus. As we have worked with people over the past two decades, we've found that evaluating these occurrences within a larger framework can provide the perspective and focus to become more efficient. We call this framework the control and importance grid, and it is the first skill in regaining balance in your life.

The grid is formed by the intersection of two variables: *control*, the extent to which you can affect a situation, and *importance*, the degree to which a matter is meaningful to you because it relates to one of your values or goals.

Situations that you face can be labeled as low importance, low control (A); high importance, low control (B); low importance, high control (C); or high importance, high control (D).

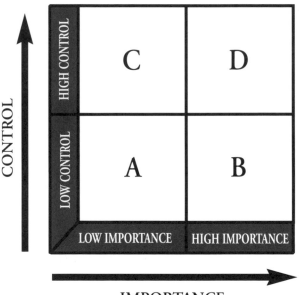

IMPORTANCE

Now let's see the grid in action.

To Achieve Balance, You've Got to Make a Match

Think back to a stressful event in your life over the past several weeks—on or off the job. As you reflect on this incident, try to remember how you reacted. Did you loose sleep over an argument with a family member, or put off an unpleasant meeting with an employee? Look back at the list of common stress-related reactions on page 48 and identify your personal reactions.

As you now consider the situation, ask yourself:
- On a scale of 1 to 10, how important was this event?
- On a scale of 1 to 10, what was my ability to control the situation?

Into which category does your scenario fit?

Low importance, low control. This is the personal equivalent of spam, the marketing emails and letters that fill our in boxes with worthless information. These items are not important enough to spend time on. Sometimes you can change them. Other times, they just keep coming back. If you want to regain life balance, spend no time on spam in its many forms. Common examples of spam are the practice of spreading rumors about people and company changes, the needless sending of emails to others, and the fixation on past mistakes at the expense of present performance.

High importance, low control. These are situations that are meaningful to you but out of your control. Many organizational decisions fall into this category. For public companies, Wall Street's valuation, while important, is independent of many leaders' performance. On a personal note, parents find themselves in this category when their child dates someone whom they don't like. What you need to recognize is that you can waste an enormous amount of time and energy in this quadrant. The antidote is to learn to let go, to recognize that you can't affect the situation, and to choose to put your energy elsewhere. Letting go is not synonymous with not caring; you still care, but for your own well-being you release your emotional attachment.

Low importance, high control. This is the busywork, the bottom items on a to-do list. Getting them done makes you feel better. This is fine if it is not done at the expense of more important items. Want to organize your computer files, get your paperwork done, call your old college friend? Go for it, just make sure it is not pulling

151

your focus from the crucial issues. Because many people have naturally high-productivity times—some in the early morning, others later in the day or at night—it is often best to attend to these issues when your natural energy levels are lower. Save the critically important items for your most productive times.

High importance, high control. These are the situations that require immediate attention. They are priorities for you or your company, and you have the power to take action to affect the outcome. If you have a crucial business presentation tomorrow, procrastination or other distractions will only cause you more distress. The situation is important, and what you do makes a real difference in your success and that of your organization. In your personal life, if your spouse or significant other lets you know that there are "major issues" that you need to discuss, again, this is the time to take immediate action and focus your attention on your relationship. When important issues collide, you may need to set aside time to address each issue separately, keeping in mind that a complex issue may have many interrelated components.

The strength of this exercise can be found with time and perspective. When you look back at a situation and your response to it, it's amazing how much smarter you can be in hindsight.

Common Energy Drains

The control-importance grid is an excellent place to start identifying energy mismatches and drains. Other drains on your time and energy include:

Personal inefficiency and disorganization. We all have periods of chaos, when we can't find anything on our desk or forget important phone calls and meetings. This is especially true for creative people, who naturally find themselves looking more to the possibilities of the future than to the minute details of the present. Not attending to important tasks and details can be a huge drain on time and energy, as we find ourselves having to recreate documents that were lost or reaffirm directions or contact information. Developing rituals for efficiency can stem such time-wasting activities. Create a to-do list with the most important items first, develop systems for record keeping (such as keeping all addresses in a special notebook or computer file), or keep a one-day diary of your activities to identify your personal time-wasters.

Not checking for understanding. The dynamics underlying most workplace communication today look like this: you're busy, they're busy. You are gearing up for "sprints," facing deadlines, and trying to juggle multiple priorities. So are your peers and subordinates. In this environment, you've got to frequently check to make sure that what *you* want, and what *they think* you want, are indeed the same thing. As the pace of change picks up, you must increasingly stop and ask the recipient "okay, repeat what I've just told you to make certain we're on the same page."

Unreal expectations. We have expectations of how we think others should perform and we have similar expectations of ourselves. These are powerful motivators of performance. They can function as good stressors that encourage subordinates and drive us to our goals. Or they can be negative stressors that result in discouragement because we can never live up to them. The problem comes when expectations are unreal or unrealistically high. When we push others or ourselves too hard, we set ourselves up for failure. Sometimes setting smaller or incremental goals, then being pleasantly surprised when they are exceeded, is the best method for successful and healthy performance in stressful times.

IDENTIFY THE SOURCES

Now that we've examined the drains on your time and attention, let's identify the sources for replenishing your energy. This search for renewal takes us full circle, because the same leadership skills that promote healthy work performance in others also help us manage ourselves. So far, we've been talking about the changes that are thrust upon us by the environment. In this section, we'll concentrate more on ways to initiate personal change to achieve greater balance.

1. Look Within Before Venturing Out

Over the past five decades, social scientists have spent considerable time creating models to explain how people make behavioral changes. Most of these models begin with a stage called consideration or contemplation. Basically, it consists of looking inward and taking stock of one's health. Some of the most successful leadership programs in which we have been involved have included executive health-risk screening. The screening includes biometric data such as height and weight, blood pressure, and serum cholesterol, along with health risk appraisals (HRAs).

HRAs are computerized assessments that examine your personal health history, heredity, and lifestyle factors and calculate your relative risk for conditions such as heart disease and cancer. The data are usually presented as a snapshot, not of your chronological age, but of your biological age. Most HRAs discuss the potential not only for turning back the clock and potentially living longer if you make some lifestyle changes, but also address your quality of life. HRA data can be powerful motivators for change, particularly in those people who exhibit a high level of denial.

While an HRA will provide quantifiable data, another way to launch the consideration phase of change involves honestly answering the following questions:

- How well do I perform when I do/don't feel well?
- How clear is my thinking and ability to focus?
- How good is my stamina?

- Am I able to handle increasing amounts of stress and change?
- What would be the cost to my organization of losing a key leader to premature disability or death?

One of the benefits of gaining greater personal insight is that it also allows for a broader understanding of the new context.

2. Clarify the New Context

To regain an element of balance and make healthy changes, you must address the new context. This entails an appreciation for what we call the health/productivity connection, revealed by your answers to the questions above. Once you're ready to look at the new rules, you can then create your personal blob diagram, following the example on page 66. No matter what balance improvement effort you choose to adopt—exercise more, spend more quality time with family, lose weight, or cut down on alcohol use—you can ask yourself:

- What is staying the same?
- What is changing?
- What do I need to let go of?
- Where do I need to reinvest?

Once you've got a handle on this, you can then go on a personal norm search. Context is defined by rules, and rules are shaped by the unwritten, popularly accepted norms of the culture. To maintain healthy practices, you'll need a more supportive culture. For example, if you choose to minimize alcohol use, you'll need a strategy to avoid excess consumption at social events and business meetings. The best way to do this is to complete the following sentence.

Around here it's normal for people (with regard to your issue) to . . .

Once you've identified the norms that can get in your way, ask yourself what you can do to change them.

155

3. Set a Direction, Even Though It's Likely to Change

Health and balance improvement is no different than business process improvement. You want to work backward from your intended destination. The mind is naturally a goal-oriented, goal-setting system. People do best when they have an endpoint to head toward, a direction in which to turn, and guideposts along the way. By setting goals, you give your mind the ability to focus and get you going in the right direction. The best goals follow the SMART plan in that they are:

Specific. Reduce your goal to writing. Avoid vagueness such as *I'd like to* or *want to*. Replace a weak goal with the words *I will*.

Measurable. Goals need to have an element of quantification. Make certain you can measure improvement.

Agreed upon. Gain the support of others. Friends, family members, and coworkers can often be enlisted to help you along the way.

Rewarding. It's helpful to build in frequent rewards and recognition to help stay on course. All good change efforts involve celebration, not only for reaching the goal, but also for reaching milestones along the way.

Trackable. Create a system to track your progress. Use graph paper or make notes in your PDA, calendar, or journal. This provides the advantage of perspective. You can look back and recognize your personal patterns.

In working through business issues, you are undoubtedly familiar with both the strength and the weakness of consensus. Getting everyone to agree on the one item or issue to be accomplished provides incredible power, but only if everyone is committed to this path. Just as we advocate that leaders never leave a consensus meeting without asking each person to rate his or her commitment (we like a scale of 1 to 10, with 10 being absolute), we also challenge individuals to evaluate their personal change goals. If, on a scale of 1 to 10, you do not give yourself a 9 or 10, then we encourage you to rework your goal statement.

4. Communicate with Credibility

Remember the ME-YOU conversations that can either help to establish or dissolve trust, depending on how open and honest you are with your emotions and disclosure? Another way to make the change process more rewarding is to make sure that the ME-ME and ME-YOU conversations are in accordance. Stress and strain occur when we say one thing and do another, or when our actions are out of step with our beliefs.

We see examples of these personal disconnects every day. In our workshops, we often ask participants whether they value their health. All the hands go up. We get universal agreement on the value of commonly heard phrases such as "health is wealth," or "without your health, what do you have?" We'll then ask seminar attendees to raise their hands if they lead a lifestyle totally in congruence with this value. Of course, no hands go up. When it comes to health and balance, all of us have a gap between our deeply held beliefs and our daily actions. The goal is to work toward closing this gap rather than allowing it to expand.

5. Take the LEAP with Your People

As we mentioned before, some of the first balls that get dropped when we're juggling too much are our relationships with friends and family. Yet it is these relationships from which we can draw strength in times of stress. Numerous studies support the link between health and personal relationships. In one nine-year study, for example, researchers found that people who had more friends had a 60 percent lower death risk compared to those with fewer personal connections. Other researchers have concluded that a lack of social ties can be as detrimental to one's health as being overweight or smoking.

And while we don't like to play up differences between men and women, there is a growing body of research that says that social relationships are especially trying and rewarding for women. First, women on average carry a larger share of family responsibilities—they miss more workdays taking care of sick children than men do and more often cite balancing work and life as a major stressor. At the same time, new research is showing how women naturally reap physiological health benefits from their personal relationships. Research on stress has found that men respond to stress with an increase in adrenaline to "fight or take flight." A recent UCLA study, on the other hand, found that one of women's responses to stress can be to produce the chemical oxytocin, which encourages the response to "tend and befriend." The more time women take to hang out with one another, the more oxytocin is released, creating a calming effect.

Friendships and personal connections are a source of strength for both men and women. By listening, empathizing, and sharing with people in difficult times, we're deepening existing relationships and creating new ones; we're generating greater intimacy. Staying connected—to friends, family, a religious community, or through civic activities—keeps us grounded, reminds us what's important, and can even keep us healthy.

6. Remember, There's Always One More Way to Look at a Situation

When it comes to trying to achieve more balance, most people get caught in ruts. They turn to the same solutions. Creative problem solving is a skill that helps to improve situations at home and at work. There are many paths that lead toward balance. If one road doesn't lead toward your goal, try another. Often it takes many attempts to discover how to overcome barriers to well-being.

Your perspective on any problem is shaped by your attitude and whether you view events with hope, optimism, and confidence, or cynicism, hostility, and anger. In order to find possibilities in life's challenges, you'll always do better with a positive perspective. Recent studies have shown that optimism promotes longevity, while anger, hostility, and cynicism are risk factors for heart disease.

CONCLUSION

In many ways, leadership in times of stress and change is all about striking an appropriate balance. Throughout this book, we've asked questions such as: Is it best to hold back or open up? Should we come up with new ideas or take immediate action? And more importantly, to what *degree* should we focus on one end of the spectrum or the other? When creating balance in our personal lives, we need to ask ourselves similar questions. Instead of choosing *either* life or work, we need to find a balance that allows us to function at our personal best. At times, we may need to put in 80-hour weeks at work, focus on the feelings of our employees, and put others before ourselves. But no one can keep up this pace for long without burning out. Balance is about looking at the big picture, making sure that overall we make time for the elements of work and life that we deem the most important.

The best and safest thing is to keep a balance in your life, acknowledge the great powers around us and in us. If you can do that, and live that way, you are really a wise man [or woman].
— *Euripides*

CONCLUSION

CHANGE LEADERSHIP

One of the first things we do when we conduct a change leadership workshop—before we get into the content and skills—is to ask people to work individually and to list the top three attributes they think a good change leader should possess. When they compare notes, there is a great deal of overlap and similarity in their answers. A typical final list indicates that good change leaders should:

- Have a vision.
- Provide motivation.
- Instill confidence.
- Create a direction.
- Provide resources.

These attributes might be characterized as the predictable skills of change leadership. People feel confident responding with these attributes because they have been told over and over that this is what leaders are supposed to do. When we go a step further and ask the participants what image corresponds to these traits, the response we often get is that of a leader riding a horse, in a tank, or driving a racecar. Each of these images connotes clearly directed forward movement and certainty.

As the workshop continues, however, the participants' perception of what is needed begins to change.

First, they start to understand that a changing environment is characterized less by clear-cut, forward movement and absoluteness of plan than by a circular and initially more inward-directed course of action. Taking this route means dealing with new factors such as lack of clarity, increasing stress and ambiguity, and a heightened need for trust and emotional support.

As the nature of this environment becomes more clear, participants also begin to see the skills of leadership more in terms of what is it like to be on the "receiving" end of change leadership. This helps them really understand and appreciate what their people need from them. As a result, the question about leadership evolves and becomes something like: What would *you* like to see in a change leader? A typical list composed by the participants now shows that a good change leader should provide:

- **Communication.**
- **Support.**
- **Openness.**
- **Empathy.**
- **Flexibility.**

In short, people begin to realize that in an environment characterized by ambiguity, change, and stress, what people look for and respond to best is someone who:

- **Lets me know what's going on and isn't afraid to say "I don't know."**
- **Is easy to "read" so I know where he or she is coming from.**
- **Sets clear expectations, ones that are sure to change and will then be replaced with *new* clear expectations.**
- **"Hears" me—is willing to listen.**
- **Demonstrates flexibility—expects and responds to turnarounds and new information.**

- Involves me and isn't afraid to ask for help.
- Is visible and available.
- Seems "together" in thought and action.

As you can see, the language in this last list is different both in content and in expression. It contains attributes that may seem a little more subjective and uses colloquial terms such as "coming from," "hears me," "read," and "together." Subjective or soft as these attributes may appear, they are not. As we have mentioned, they have a steel core running through them. Indeed, they require more courage and skills to apply than the controlled, logical attributes of the first list. In contrast to the knight on the white horse who charges in, attacking everything in sight, this new change leader is more of a mentor. Think back to someone who has inspired you in the past—a coach, teacher, religious leader, or friend. You appreciated their advice or leadership because they listened, you trusted them, and they cared.

In the introduction, we merged these values into what we called the three key attributes for change leadership:

- Flexibility.
- Empathy.
- Trustworthiness.

When you first read them, they may have just seemed like nice words on a piece of paper—like motherhood and apple pie. Or you may have asked yourself, who *wouldn't* do these things?

Hopefully, now you see them in a different light—as a compact summary of a larger set of critical skills for leading in times of stress and change.

The Giuliani Factor

In the middle of the process of putting this book together, we happened to be looking at the *Time Magazine* "Person of the Year" issue applauding New

York Mayor Rudy Giuliani for his leadership after September 11. We were immediately struck by the fact that the issue was a veritable textbook for how to lead in times of crisis and change. You don't even have to read the text, the pictures tell it all: The mayor in his SUV mobile office, directing the rescue and recovery effort; the mayor bent in grief with his hands folded at a funeral; the mayor walking the talk at "Ground Zero," talking to his people, giving and asking for advice; the mayor embracing a widow amid the wreckage; the mayor revealing his own hopes and fears, and then clowning it up on *Saturday Night Live.*

The article lauded his candor, his heart, his firm direction, his compassion, his capacity to listen, his courage, his ability to change direction, and his willingness to have fun. In short, Giuliani:

- **Showed determination and resolve.**
- **Defined outcomes and set a direction.**
- **Managed his inner turmoil and sense of loss.**
- **Demonstrated vulnerability and compassion.**
- **"Let his hair down" and gave people permission to laugh.**

Whatever one thinks of Giuliani's politics, and whatever he does in the future, during this time of national grief and stress he took the skills of empathy, flexibility, and trustworthiness, as well as establishing a firm direction and purpose, to their highest levels. We found in his example strong support for our own conclusions about what a good change leader is all about.

The Good News and the Bad News

In terms of the skills presented in this book:

- The good news is that they *work*—they're not always easy, but they *do* work.
- The bad news is that they only work with "normal" people.

Some people, no matter what you do, no matter how hard you try, are going to stay upset, resist new things, refuse to be flexible, blow off your attempts to support them, demand consistency and control, and, in general, behave like victims.

These people are on what we call "the other side of the line." Your efforts and our skills are not going to reach them.

Luckily, these "abnormal" people are only a minuscule percent of the population. The remainder—although they may seem abnormal at times—will respond to the skills we have presented here. They'll play fair.

We hope you have found the insights and skills in this book both valuable and applicable. We invite you to try them out in your own changing environments.

SUPPORTING RESEARCH

Our work in *Leadership in Times of Stress and Change* is based not only on a combined four decades of experience, but also on in-depth research into the nature of change. Following are some of the major studies and surveys that have influenced our work. Most are from the past two years; some are as recent as the month we went to publication. The introduction and each of the seven skills, chapters 1 through 7, are addressed separately, but there's a common theme that comes through in the data: Change has become the norm rather than the exception, and the companies that succeed in turbulent times are those that listen and communicate, and thus inspire confidence and loyalty in their employees.

Introduction

Do you feel overworked, under-appreciated, and stressed out? If your answer is yes, then you're in good company. In a study conducted by the Families and Work Institute, almost half of respondents said they felt overworked in one way or another. Life in the 21st century is full of long hours at work, tiring commutes, and input overload. Two recent quality-of-life surveys found that:

- Approximately one-quarter of employees in the U.S. work 50 or more hours per week, spend six or seven days a week at work, and don't use all of their vacation time.
- Between one-third and one-half of respondents said they often felt overworked, overwhelmed, and that they didn't have time to step back and reflect on their work.
- Overworked employees are more likely to make mistakes, be angry with their employers, and seek a new job. Seventeen percent of people who felt overworked said they often made mistakes at work,

while only one percent of those who did not feel overwhelmed said they often made mistakes.

In many ways, technology has made work more all-consuming, rather than easier. Cell phones, pagers, email, and laptop computers make it harder to get away from the "office," even when on vacation. A recent study of internet users by Gartner Inc., a market research firm, found that:

- **A quarter of respondents check their business email on weekends, and a full 42 percent check email while on vacation.**
- **Workers received an average of 22 emails per day. Continually checking for and reading new emails takes up valuable time at work, almost an hour a day on average. More than half of people check email six or more times a day, while a third of users say they look "constantly."**
- **Only 27 percent of business emails require imme-diate attention, while more than a third of emails are "occupational spam," a term the survey used to denote unnecessary emails from coworkers.**

According to Maurene Caplan Grey of Gartner, Inc., "Business use of cell phones, instant messaging, and email has crept into our lives on a 24 by seven basis. The connected vacationer is always on the alert for business interruptions."

All of this stress can take its toll on companies, in more ways than we think. According to a study of near-ly 50,000 employees, which was published in the *American Journal of Health Promotion*, stress is the most expensive preventable health risk that organizations face.

So how do business leaders combat the ever-expand-ing workweek? A 2002 survey by the Center for Creative Leadership found that it's the "soft skills" that make a difference in tough times. The center asked 77 business leaders to assess what worked best during changing times and what didn't. The two skills consistently associated with positive change leaders were:

- **Honest, proactive communication.**
- **Good listening, sensitivity, and the willingness to clearly articulate the rationale and necessity for change.**

"Effective leaders seem better at blending the softer leadership skills—trust, empathy, and genuine communication—with the tough skills needed to keep an organization afloat during difficult times," said Kerry Bunker of the Center. "In contrast, our survey showed that ineffective leaders were poor communicators who were insensitive to employee needs and who were generally inaccessible."

In a similar survey, the Atlanta Chapter of the Society for Human Resource Management (SHRM) found that the number one skill for managers during times of turmoil was flexibility.

While work may seem overwhelming, the skills of communication and flexibility can help you to help your people during difficult times.

Chapter 1: Look Within Before Venturing Out

The value of self-reflection is a core theme in many stress-management programs. The Peter F. Drucker Foundation for Nonprofit Management is one of the most well-known proponents of organizational introspection, assessment, and vision. Frances Hesselbein, chairman of the Drucker Foundation and former chief executive of the Girl Scouts of America, spoke of the value of "cleaning house" in a recent article—cleaning out closets and attics, stepping back and assessing what is worth keeping, what works, and what doesn't. She called on leaders to ask several questions of their organizations including:

- What are our leadership strengths?
- What are areas to be strengthened?
- How do we deploy our leaders, our teams, our people to further the mission and achieve our goals?
- Do our leaders see themselves as the embodiment of the mission, values, and beliefs of the organization?
- How can we sharpen communication skills and attitudes—knowing that communication is not merely saying something, it is being heard?

Hesselbein also advocates *personal* reflection to make sure that our values and vision for ourselves are in line with the mission of our organization.

Today's organizational managers aren't the originators of placing an emphasis on self-reflection. Renowned psychologist William James argued more than a century ago that "introspective observation is what we have to rely on first and foremost and always." In the 1970s, Albert Bandura, the father of Social Cognitive Theory, addressed the causal relation between self-reflection and action—that humans are self-regulating individuals who reflect and process information, rather than being at the whims of the external environment. In fact, Bandura said that the ability to self-reflect and then modify behavior is a large part of what makes us human.

All of these methods of introspection share commonalties: Reflection is seen as a positive step in the change process; it is also seen as a great moment for learning, as we survey what is occurring, what we've done in the past, and what the future might bring.

Take, for example, the case of a group of Colorado librarians who came together in 1997 for a series of workshops designed to enhance their skills and develop an internal locus of control—to understand that the effectiveness of their performance could be attributed largely to factors under their own command. In a follow-up survey six months later:

- Almost all participants (95 percent) said they were more inclined to see matters as within their own control.
- Eighty-five percent said they were more likely to set work-related goals and objectives.
- Two-thirds reported that they were developing customer service procedures for their library programs.
- Finally, 90 percent of participants reported improved communication with their coworkers and about half said they were involved more frequently in innovative decision making.

The power of self-reflection—the skill of looking within before venturing outward and acknowledging your own control over the situation—is an essential first step not only of a positive change process, but of any adventure.

Chapter 2: Clarify the New Context

Change has become a "normal" part of organizational structure. According to the U.S. Department of Labor, almost 15,000 companies laid off at least 50 people in 1999. The Society for Human Resource Management found that *almost half* of companies they surveyed had laid off employees in 2000 and the first part of 2001. In their "Layoffs and Job Security Survey," SHRM confirmed that restructuring and layoffs have a negative effect on employee moral and retention:

- Employee morale decreased for 58 percent of respondents.
- Gossip increased in 54 percent of cases.
- Forty-one percent said company loyalty diminished.
- More than a quarter of the companies reported an increase in resignations.

In technology organizations, more than two thirds of employees have either been laid off or have seen friends and coworkers let go in the past three years, according to a new survey of 1600 tech employees. A common response to such restructuring, the study found, is a decrease in company loyalty and to "assume all jobs are temporary." Furthermore, in a study of job involvement during restructuring, the insecurity of change was directly related to:

- **Decreased job satisfaction.**
- **Greater incidence of health problems.**
- **Increased work and task withdrawal, absenteeism, and a greater likelihood of quitting.**
- **Higher psychological distress.**

The negative effects that change can have on employees can be expensive. Estimates to replace an employee, including training and recruitment, easily reach as high as 70 to 80 percent of their annual salary. There's also lower productivity during the training period for both the new hire and the managers, and a higher stress level for those who remain.

All in all, in changing times, managers may have a difficult road ahead, one made easier if they can work to clarify the context of the changes and help keep employee loyalty and productivity on target.

Chapter 3: Set a Direction, Even Though It's Likely to Change

There is an inordinate amount of literature that relates goal setting to motivation. If an employee "buys in" to a goal—if they are committed to reach it—then they are more likely to work harder to attain the objective, whether it's actually reachable or not. A group of researchers from Ohio State and Michigan State universities conducted a review of nearly 100 separate goal-setting studies and concluded that:

- Goals are a central force in work motivation.
- The more committed a person is to a goal, the higher their motivation and performance will be.
- The difficulty of the objective does not hinder motivation.

It should be clear that abandoning goal setting during times of change is not the solution for employee motivation. Yet holding rigidly to an unchanging objective will also spell disaster. A better solution——one that combines having an objective with the reality of a constantly changing environment—is to set a direction or target, and then work backward from that goal.

The idea of working backward from a target is a component of *systems thinking*. Systems thinking, first articulated by Ludwig von Bertalanffy in 1950, takes a more holistic, adaptive look at organizations, studying the entire situation instead of addressing parts separately. The problem with traditional goal setting is that issues are defined too narrowly, the goal is static, and the causes and connections of the problem are not addressed. Goals may be modified slightly along the route, but any change in context is not taken into account—that is, change in intention, approach, or the business or company environment. Systems thinking, on the other hand, sees an organization as an open system in which goals are modified through feedback and allowed to grow, adapt, and expand. This is the basis of "the learning organization."

The scout model of change put forth in *Leadership* builds on the strengths of systems thinking. It works backward to move forward, receives regular feedback, and is adaptive.

Chapter 4: Communicate with Credibility

In survey after survey, employees consistently rank trust and loyalty the most important values in the workplace. Two major studies conducted by human resources companies in 2000-2001 found that:

- Between 91 and 99 percent of employees said that workplace trust was an important factor, yet only 29 percent felt that they currently had a high level of trust within their company.
- Trust ranked as the third most important value for employees, ranking higher than salary. (Work-life balance and meaningfulness of work were the top two.)
- Only 6 percent of human resource managers, on the other hand, listed lack of trust as one of the main reasons that employees resigned.

This lack of trust has been growing over the past two decades. Restructuring, layoffs, and rapid changes mean that employees no longer get, nor expect, a "lifetime of work for loyalty." Just over half of employees say they feel a sense of loyalty or commitment to their employers—down 7 percent from 10 years ago. Why is this the case? Employees fear being laid off without notice—and for good reason. In a study of 572 human resource professionals, the Society for Human Resource Management found that 43 percent of companies with layoffs gave no notice at all.

A lack of honesty and disclosure adds to the tension. Almost two-thirds of tech employees, in a recent survey, said that industry instability had increased their sense of distrust and negative feelings about work. Ten percent agreed with the most extreme statement, "I no longer trust my employer; I'll do my job but as soon as another job comes along, I'm gone." SHRM found that communication and understanding is one of the best ways to limit the negative effects of major changes. When people understood and felt comfortable with the reasons for the changes, they were more accepting of the layoffs and less likely to have a decrease in employee loyalty.

Being honest, sharing your feelings, and showing concern are some of the best ways to instill trust.

Chapter 5: Take the LEAP with Your People

The top three skills that leaders need to work on, according to a recent global study of 10,000 employees, are: fairness at work, care and concern for employees, and trust. Yet leaders often have a skewed view of the importance of care and concern, either believing that the level between employee and manager is higher than it is, or downplaying its value.

In a national study, business executives listed the top personal traits they believed made a good leader; commutation skills, integrity, and vision topped the list. Empathy, however—one of the traits employees most desire in their managers—was at the bottom of the list for these executives, scoring a mere 6 percent. Ironically, the majority of these executives cited employee retention as a major concern and identified part of the cause as employee lack of company loyalty.

This gap also exists within levels of management. An Australian survey of 500 major companies found:

- **Twenty percent of chief executives said that worker morale was excellent; only 6 percent of managers agreed.**
- **The majority of CEOs said that stress reduction programs were in place; yet a third of senior managers said their company had done nothing to alleviate stress.**
- **Eighty-three percent of chief executives thought that their development programs improved employee morale and retention; a mere 18 percent of managers were of the same opinion.**

The relationship between leaders and employees is an important one. It consistently ranks as one of the top workplace values for employees. And a positive approach to leadership, one that involves the skills of empathy, listening, and support, is the key to strengthening that relationship.

Chapter 6: Remember, There's Always One More Way to Look at a Situation

Creativity is vital to business success, and the majority of managers agree, says an American Express survey of 300 small-business owners. Nearly all (96 percent) said that creative ideas are "crucial," "very important," or "important" to their business success, and more than half say that their employees come up with the best ideas. A third of new ideas, they say, are formed outside of the office, at informal gatherings, networking, or "out of the blue."

Yet many business leaders set aside very little time for developing creative ideas. And tight deadlines are the number one block for creativity, according to a 2001 survey of marketing and advertising companies. Other creative blocks include:

- **Lack of inspiration.**
- **Stress.**
- **Long hours.**
- **Fatigue.**
- **Lack of clear direction.**
- **Lack of information.**

The best way to overcome a creative block, according to respondents, was to take a break from the project or task.

Bill Lucas, chief executive of the Campaign for Learning, has found that the right combination of stress and challenge is the best way to stimulate the brain. But if the brain is pushed too hard, he says, even a simple task can be difficult or impossible.

Brainstorming, long known to be a positive process for stimulating creativity, works best when the brain isn't

pushed too hard to work under pressure or within deadlines. When combined with a mental break, feedback,
and openness to ideas "out of the blue," strong ideas that
stay strong over time and help the company are the
result.

Chapter 7: Keep Balance in Mind

Work-life balance is consistently ranked as one of the
most important factors in job satisfaction and the top of
the benefits wish list:

- The importance of a work-life balance was spontaneously mentioned by 30 percent of respondents
  in a 1999 survey of young professionals, from 600
  companies across 73 countries. In the U.S., it was
  the number one career value.
- Achieving a greater work-life balance was most
  important to baby boomers, according to a poll of
  2600 employees at the end of 2000.
- Balance and flexibility is especially important for
  women. In a survey of IT women, about two
  thirds said that work had a negative effect on their
  personal lives and they felt stressed by a work-life
  imbalance.

When work interferes with life, a variety of negative
results occur:

- Diminished job and career satisfaction.
- Low levels of quality of life.
- Negative behaviors at work such as increased
  harassment and incivility.
- Increased incidence of work withdrawal.
- Higher levels of stress.

Furthermore, as work-life programs have been implemented throughout the 1980s, 1990s, and today, sub-
stantial data have accumulated that creating greater
work-life balance is actually good for business.
Numerous recent studies have found that:

- According to three-quarters of managers, work-life programs did not lead to any additional increase in cost, or the costs were minimal.
- Benefits included a happier staff, increased employee retention, and reduced absenteeism levels.
- Managers overwhelming agreed that employees worked better when they could balance work and life (91 percent); had more motivation and commitment to the company (58 percent), and were happier with employment relations (72 percent).

Still not convinced that finding a positive work-life balance is better for your company and your personal well-being? Consider the case of Arnold & Porter, a law firm in Washington, D.C. By helping employees find back-up childcare and sick care, they reduced the number of absences and saved $800,000 in one year. Aetna, in an attempt to retain employees lost to family concerns, makes it easier for women to return part-time after childbirth and saved $1 million to $2 million annually. Finally, nearly two-thirds of 800 employers representing 7 million workers said that their work-life programs had lifted morale.

Part of obtaining balance involves discovering which areas of work and life need the most improvement. A number of companies provide comprehensive health risk appraisals and summary reports. These include InfoTech (www.wellnesscheckpoint.com), Staywell (www.staywell.com), Johnson & Johnson Health Care Systems (www.jjhcshealth-fitness.com), Wellsource (www.wellsource.com), and RealAge (www.realage.com).

One of the advantages of summary data is that you can compare your organization's health risks against national norms. Often, the health risks in populations of executives parallel those in the general population, once they have been adjusted for race, gender, education, and age. Consider a few of the following statistics for the United States:

- A quarter of men between the ages of 35 and 44 have engaged in binge drinking in the past month (consumption of five or more drinks on at least one occasion). For women of the same age group, the total is 7.8 percent. Over the next 10 years, the percent goes down to 12.2 for men and 2.9 for women.

- Twenty-three percent of Americans ages 20–74 have hypertension, 19 percent have high cholesterol.

- About a fifth of Americans are technically obese.

Risk factors in the Canadian population are similar to those in the U.S.:

- Forty-eight and forty-three percent of men and women, respectively, have elevated total plasma cholesterol.

- Fifteen percent of Canadians have high blood pressure and/or are undergoing medical treatment for it.

- A quarter of the population with high blood pressure are unaware of their condition. Of those who are aware, just over half have received treatment to bring their blood pressure under control.

- Thirty-one percent of Canadian adults are considered obese (using a lower figure than the U.S. does to define obesity).

STORIES OF EXCEPTIONAL LEADERS

As we completed the writing of *Leadership in Times of Stress and Change*, we encouraged a number of our colleagues from the Society for Human Resource Management (SHRM) to review several chapters of the book. We asked them if they knew of any leaders who exemplified some of the seven skills presented. We also asked for personal tips, hints, and techniques that they had found helpful in negotiating turbulent organizational waters. The responses we received were incredibly helpful and reiterate how valuable a strong leader is to an organization in duress. We culled these responses from the more than 100 we received. Apologies are extended to those who sent us examples but did not get included. Many of your comments were integrated into the text.

From: "Maudie Holm" <MHOLM@plaind.com>
To: <mtager@workskills-lifeskills.com>
Sent: April 24, 2002
Subject: Comments on "Leadership"

One more way—Always, always, always be open to this possibility. I worked for a stellar boss (and mentor) years ago and his philosophy regarding customer service was this: "There is no such answer as 'no.'" Rich Koeller, TRW Inc. (early 1980s). Awesome guy and we would go to the wall for him. With that philosophy, one had to re-think every option repeatedly or find new ones that fit our business paradigm, fit our budgetary restrictions, etc. and still come up with "yes." This remains at the heart of my service philosophy.

I sent out a quickie survey to some friends of mine re: leadership. All of these women enjoyed being mentored by others. Three commented that their mentors did not give them verbal advice as much as they led by example. Each commented that her boss "walked the talk and didn't ask me to do anything he wouldn't do himself." A com-

183

ment from Maggie McMillan Bilyk, "The boss that inspired me didn't preach a philosophy. He led by example. He generously shared everything he had learned—admitted that he was still learning—and encouraged the younger employees to question and learn and share with each other—and him. He was so proud of our successes, no matter how big or small; and this was long before employee involvement was the buzz phrase." His name was Nick LaRich, Sales Manager for WHK/WMMS Radio (1965-1975).

From another Rich Koeller mentee: "Perception is all there is." Rich Koeller (Ms. Marilyn Schager Baker.) I have a bias, since I do this, "Work backward in order to move forward." Do it all the time—it works!

From: "Anderson, Belinda"
To: <mtager@workskills-lifeskills.com>
Sent: April 02, 2002
Subject: Comments on "Leadership"

I worked with an excellent leader who followed the "scout" concept. The 1980s was a time of many cutbacks and layoffs in the manufacturing world. Employees were scared, angry and confused. John had been in Human Resources his entire career and saw an opportunity to apply his "people skills" to the operations of this manufacturing organization. In making the change from Human Resources to Operations, John was satisfying one of his personal goals to apply his "human relations" skills to the operations of the company to positively affect the bottom line during these turbulent times and make employees feel good about themselves.

He listened to all employees; he set up work groups; he showed all employees that he had faith in them; and he established trustworthiness with all levels of employees. The employees knew the desired outcomes and expectations, but he allowed them to chart their own course. He was always there for them giving them support, updates and encouragement as they progressed. Because it was a manufacturing organization, the employees worked on various components of the finished product, but never got to see the finished product. John listened to this concern and arranged tours for the employees so they could see what they had accomplished. The sense of pride that evolved was immeasurable. His leadership inspired employees to be committed, dedicated, and energized. He helped them to feel good about their jobs again and take pride in their work. Despite the inevitable staff reductions, the bottom line was positive and the work environment was positive due to his strong leadership skills.

My personal style is to inform and explain to employees what we are trying to accomplish. I then open the communication channels for them to deliver their input and ideas. We all brainstorm the options and start moving in the desired direction. But most importantly, everyone knows we can talk, meet--whatever--whenever it becomes necessary because of unexpected factors. The icing on the cake is the unexpected rewards to the staff as we proceed along our journeys. It might be a special email; a handwritten note; appropriate acknowledgement at a staff meeting --just to send the message that I do care and do appreciate their work and their commitment. It keeps them motivated to move forward. I see myself as a teacher, a guide--always there as a safety net for them.

I tell my staff that my own success depends on their success, and I will do whatever it takes to help them be successful.

From: "Lindh, Debra"
To: <mtager@workskills-lifeskills.com>
Sent: April 04, 2002
Subject: Comments on "Leadership"

I am aware of two people who are extraordinary examples of leaders successfully guiding people. One individual is Julie Streeter Dallin. I have had the pleasure of working with Julie. Julie is the type of leader written about in *Leadership in Times of Stress and Change*. She is a leader who stands behind her people, coaches, mentors, possesses the highest integrity, encourages her people to think outside the box, means what she says, explains why things need to be done (so you understand business, not that it's just the way it's going to be) and she is always going the extra mile. One of the things I enjoy most about Julie is her contagious energy. She has a way about her that makes you discover things about yourself that you never thought were possible. She is the type of leader and boss that people wish they had.

Another person who I know who is an extraordinary example of a leader successfully guiding people is Dr. Michael Jones. I have had the pleasure of knowing Michael for several years. Michael is the type of leader who challenges the "whole you." His method of challenge results in self-awareness, examination of your world views, exploration of beliefs, knowledge, truth, and life. The things I enjoy most about Michael are his wisdom and honesty. His honesty is Scorpion-like, but is necessary for self-development and is always expressed with compassion. Michael has impacted and brought about change in many lives and shares his time with many people.

From: "Anderson, Kathy" <kathyanderson@aha.org>
To: <mtager@workskills-lifeskills.com>
Sent: April 05, 2002
Subject: Comments on "Leadership"

Regarding examples of leaders who have successfully led groups in challenging times, I'd use my own manager, AHA's Vice-President of HR, as an example. She was able to come in during a very uncertain time, identify and address HR and organizational issues, and lead the HR team in identifying the "hows and whys" of setting HR goals that aligned with organizational goals. She continues to demonstrate leadership skills that all AHA staff, particularly the HR team, can aspire to.

The biggest tip that I can give regarding leading others

through challenging times is to model the behavior you expect of others, but do so in an open and honest manner. This means acknowledging your own as well as other's feelings, issues and concerns in a positive way.

From: "Colon, Mike", mike.colon@mail.co.ventura.ca.us
To: <mtager@workskills-lifeskills.com>
Sent: March 31, 2002
Subject: Comments on "Leadership"

The most visible leader in my field in terms of providing leadership in times of change is the former commissioner of the New York City Police Department, William "Bill" Bratton. Commissioner Bratton's cutting-edge policing strategies brought about historic reductions in New York City's crime rate. Another good example is Superintendent Richard Pennington of the New Orleans Police Department. Mr. Pennington took over a very corrupt police department and changed it around.

On a personal note my experience and education has taught me that successful leaders never stop learning from every experience and from every person they work with regardless of rank or standing. Expectations should be clear, promoted, compelling, and most importantly adjusted to your strategy. Commitment should be public and acceptable with or without risk. Being positive and enthusiastic is just as important as having good people skills.

From: "Mercer, Cynthia" <cmercer@oakwood.com>
To: <mtager@workskills-lifeskills.com>
Sent: April 09, 2002
Subject: Comments on "Leadership"

Oakwood Worldwide is a privately owned and operated organization that has been in business for over 40 years. Our Chairman, Howard Ruby is the epitome of an extraordinary leader. Following the events of 9/11, Mr. Ruby quickly stepped into action. The initial response was to ensure the safety and security of our employees and customers. A letter from the Chairman was sent to all employees and customers prior to close of business on 9/11. The message was that of support, empathy, and a commitment for continued communication. The days that followed were met with ongoing communication that ranged from charitable efforts, time off for mourning, and the deployment of counseling services. A concerted effort was made to ensure that our employees were given the information, compassion and hopes to move forward. When the timing was right, Mr. Ruby gently called us to action. Through empathetic and supportive messages, we declared a call to action. Mr. Ruby fostered a spirit of pride in our country and our company that is rare and contagious.

Through layoffs, budget cuts, and minimal salary increases, we have seen very little voluntary turnover. Why? Because we have a leader that is open, honest and able to engage 3,000 people toward a common cause.

From: "Eads, Vickie"
To: <mtager@workskills-lifeskills.com>
Sent: March 27, 2002
Subject: Comments on "Leadership"

I can recount a truly successful change experience that mirrored much of what you described. I worked for a large savings and loan institution that was forced by economics and competition to significantly modify the lending side of the operation. This meant moving from an environment of 100+ "full service" field offices to less than 80 Point of Sale locations supported by two large, central operating units that provided all of the back office and administrative support following a sale. We identified the ultimate goal early on--some two years before we intended to complete the initiative. The initial announcement did result in significant concern on the part of the employees--knowing that some would be laid off during the process and many others required to relocate and learn new skill-sets. We then established a "skunks work" environment where all members of the core project team were housed in a single location, readily available for ad hoc meetings to discuss issues, concerns, and outcomes, allowing us to modify our plan, and in some cases, portions of the final outcome/destination early on in the process.

We met and/or communicated regularly with the field office employees to let them know what we knew when we knew it. They often felt we knew more than we were prepared to tell them, but that was rarely the case. It took some time for the employees to trust that we were keeping them apprised of the real situation and progress of the project, but in time, as we linked more and more of them into the process, trust developed.

In the end, we successfully implemented the two sites and were pleased (and frankly surprised) by the small percentage of fallout that we experienced during the project. We did see peaks and valleys in performance, but we continually recognized and rewarded the peaks, and addressed the performance issues in a timely manner. The executive team that sponsored the initiative, as well as the core project team members, did an extraordinary job of guiding the people and the organization as a whole through very challenging times. Without consciously acknowledging it, I believe they clearly took the High Confidence/Low Certainty position of, "We've never done this before, but together we can get through it," and it truly paid off.

As a recap of the experience I had in my former life, I believe success in leading others through challenging times is rooted in honest communication, trusting in the support and skills of those around you, and the openness to new ideas, re-routing your course as needed, and the acknowledging that there is likely "more than one way to get there from here."

From: "Stephanie Curran" <stephanie.curran
        @mmclp.com>
To: mtager@workskills-lifeskills.com
Sent: April 2, 2002
Subject: Comments on "Leadership"

The current, new FBI director fits your example. I think of the challenges he's had to overcome entering into his new leadership role. Morale, disorganization, bad press (Ruby Ridge, Waco, McVeigh files, missing weapons and computers) then WHAM! September 11. He leads his team into unchartered waters while setting up new approaches to new problems, funding issues, and safety concerns. Knowing people who work in the FBI, I can tell you that they're stepping up to the plate and I think his leadership has plenty to do with it.

Flexibility, Empathy, Trustworthiness

They seem obvious, but it's amazing how many leaders undermine the above. They make decisions that cause their teams to see them as lacking in the last two, while expecting the team to surpass in the first. It's all got to be there in the leader for the rest of the team to have them all grow.

My tip is to overcommunicate (during change) to the point where you think people are sick of hearing from you, then you are beginning to approach the level of there being "enough" communication.

From: "Hoag, Jon" <jhoag@ded.mail.state.mo.us>
To: mtager@workskills-lifeskills.com
Sent: April 5, 2002
Subject: Comments on "Leadership"

Our department recently shifted our performance appraisal method to one that focuses on broad outcomes. Employees are asked to develop strategies that will contribute to the identified outcomes. The planning or developing of strategies is fluid, so changes to the document are expected throughout the year. The hope is to eventually change the mindset through this approach. We have a long way to go and reading your materials made me think we should share current literature on leadership with the managers/leaders of our department.

From: "Featherston, Shawn" <sfeatherston
@chronimed.com>
To: mtager@workskills-lifeskills.com
Sent: March 20, 2002
Subject: Comments on "Leadership"

In my own experience, I have found that one has to master the art of emotional stability and control, even when that is seemingly impossible to do--there is a calming effect, as your book mentions, but I don't know of a magic formula to gain the ability to do this. It seems to be intuitive--you have it or you don't, it's a rare person who can learn this, but I think it can be learned through careful observation and experience. The only other thing right off the cuff is that I have found that leaders in tough times need to be "presidential," exuding confidence regardless of the negativity of current events. You saw this with President Bush recently, and I recall observing how much in command, how confident the military leadership appeared during the Gulf War.

SELECTED REFERENCES

Following are the references for the facts and figures cited throughout the book. Whenever possible, we've also included a web site address to make the information more accessible.

Adair, Connie. "The Cost of Loyalty." *Your Office* [ca. 2001]. www.youroffice.ca.

Anderson, D., R. Whitmer, and R. Goetzel, et al. "The Relationship Between Modifiable Health Risks and Group-Level Health Care Expenditures." *American Journal of Health Promotion* 15, no. 1 (2000): 45-52.

Atella, Michael D. "Case Studies in the Development of Organizational Hardiness: From Theory to Practice." *Consulting Psychology Journal: Practice and Research* 51, no. 2 (1999): 125-134.

Blanchard, Kenneth H., et al. *Whale Done!: The Power of Positive Relationships*. New York: Free Press, 2002.

Blanchard, Kenneth H. *The Heart of a Leader*. Tulsa, Okla.: Honor Books, 1999.

Bond, Frank W., and David Bunce. "Job Control Mediates Change in a Work Reorganization Intervention for Stress Reduction." *Journal of Occupational Health Psychology* 6, no. 4 (2001): 290-302.

Britt, Thomas W., Amy B. Adler, and Paul T. Bartone. "Deriving Benefits from Stressful Events: The Role of Engagement in Meaningful Work and Hardiness." *Journal of Occupational Health Psychology* 6, no. 1 (2001): 53-63.

"Business Ideas Can Spring from Anywhere—Even Out of the Blue." 28 June 2000. www.bankrate.com.

Canadian Heart Health Initiative. "Heart Disease & Stroke in Canada." 1995. http://www.med.mun.ca/chhdbc/.

The Career Innovation Research Group. "Riding the Wave: The New Global Career Culture." 1999. www.careerinnovation.com.

Centers for Disease Control. "Behavioral Risk Factor Surveillance System." 1999. www.cdc.gov/nccdphp/brfss/.

Cortina, Lila M., Vicki J. Magley, Jill Hunter Williams, and Regina Day Langhout. "Incivility in the Workplace: Incidence and Impact." *Journal of Occupational Health Psychology* 6, no. 1 (2001): 64-80.

The Creative Group. "Slow Down! Survey Shows Tight Deadlines Most Common Cause of Creative Blocks." 26 July 2001. www.creativegroup.com.

Department of Trade and Industry, United Kingdom. "Work-Life Balance – Key Facts." www.dti.gov.uk/.

"Digital Economy May Change, But Attributes of Leaders Don't, According to A.T. Kearney Survey." 8 November 2000. www.atkearney.com.

Edmonds, Patricia, and Anna Braasch. "Workplace Shakeups Shatter Trust." 2001. home.techies.com.

Greenhaus, Jeffrey H., Saroj Parasuraman, and Karen M. Collins. "Career Involvement and Family

Involvement as Moderators of Relationships between Work-Family Conflict and Withdrawal from a Profession." *Journal of Occupational Health Psychology* 6, no. 2 (2001): 91-100.

Hechanova-Alampay, Regina, and Terry A. Beehr. "Empowerment, Span of Control, and Safety Performance in Work Teams after Workforce Reduction." *Journal of Occupational Health Psychology* 6, no. 4 (2001): 275-282.

Hesselbein, Frances. "Putting One's House in Order." *Leader to Leader*, no. 16 (2000).

"How Employers are Handling Layoffs, and their Aftermath." *HR Focus* 79, no. 2 (2002): 8.

Human Resources Development Canada. "The Business Case for Work-Life Balance." 20 February 2002, http://labour.hrdc-drhc.gc.ca/worklife/businesscase-en.cfm.

Judge, Timothy A., Carl J. Thoresen, Joyce E. Bono, and Gregory K. Patton. "The Job-Satisfaction-Job Performance Relationship: A Qualitative and Quantitative Review." *Psychological Bulletin* 127, no. 3 (2001): 376-407.

Kavanagh, John. "Human frailty: Australian Executives Are Falling Behind in the 'Soft' Issues of Human Resources and Succession Management." *BRW* (7-13 March 2002): 66-68.

Klein, Howard J., Michael J. Wesson, John R. Hollenbeck, and Bradley J. Alge. "Goal Commitment and the Goal-Setting Process: Conceptual Clarification and Empirical Synthesis." *Journal of Applied Psychology* 84, no. 6 (1999): 885-896.

"Labor Day Survey Uncovers Myths About Keeping Great Employees." 25 August 2000. www.ddiworld.com.

Langdon, Jerry. "Owners Try to Make Time for Brainstorming." *The Cincinnati Enquirer*. 6 August 2000. http://enquirer.com.

Lankarge, Vicki. "Keeping Workers and Cutting Costs Top Employers' Benefits Wish List." 20 November 2001. www.insure.com.

Lee, Kibeom, Julie J. Carswell, and Natalie J. Allen. "A Meta-Analytic Review of Occupational Commitment: Relations with Person- and Work Related Variables." *Journal of Applied Psychology* 85, no. 5 (October 2000): 799-811.

Mader, Becca. "What Do Job Seekers Want?: Trust, Stability, Personal Satisfaction Top a 2,600-Person Survey." [Milwaukee] *Business Journal*. 11 January 2002. http://milwaukee.bizjournals.com.

Martinez, Michelle. "Work-Life Programs Reap Business Benefits." *HR Magazine* (June 1997). www.shrm.org/hrmagazine.

Melymuka, Kathleen. "Stressed-Out IT Women Tempted to Quit, Survey Finds." *Computerworld*. 15 March 2001. www.infoworld.com.

Myers, George, Jr. "A Matter of Trust: Companies Searching for Ways to Strengthen Bonds with Employees." *The Columbus Dispatch*. 6 August 2000. www.bbsicareers.com.

National Center for Health Statistics, United States. 2001. www.cdc.gov/nchs/.

Pajares, Frank. "Overview of Social Cognitive Theory and of Self-Efficacy." 2002. www.emory.edu/EDU-CATION/mfp/eff.html.

Parker, Sharon K., Carolyn M. Axtell, and Nick Turner. "Designing a Safer Workplace: Importance of Job Autonomy, Communication Quality, and Supportive Supervisors." *Journal of Occupational Health Psychology* 6, no. 3 (2001): 211-228.

Probst, Tahira M. "Wedded to the Job: Moderating Effects of Job Involvement on the Consequences of Job Insecurity." *Journal of Occupational Health Psychology* 5, no. 1 (2000): 63-73.

"Programs to Balance Work, Family Lift Worker Morale." *St. Louis Business Journal.* 28 March 1997. http://stlouis.bizjournals.com.

Restak, Richard. *Mozart's Brain and the Fighter Pilot: Unleashing Your Brain's Potential.* New York: Harmony Books, 2001.

"Survey: Tight Deadlines Cause Creative Blocks." *San Jose Business Journal.* 30 July 2001. http://sanjose.bizjournals.com.

"The Third National Health and Nutrition Examination Survey." (1988-1994). http://www.cdc.gov/nchs/nhanes.htm.

INDEX

ABOUT THE AUTHORS

Harry L. Woodward, Ph.D.

Harry Woodward is a management consultant, author, and speaker. He works primarily in the areas of leadership, change management, innovation, and learning. He has consulted with and developed programs and seminars for such clients as Alcoa, IBM, General Motors, AT&T, Chase Manhattan Bank, The Chicago Mercantile Exchange, The Mayo Clinic, Nike, Prudential Insurance, Accenture, Dun & Bradstreet, Marriott, DuPont, Hewlett Packard, Genentech, and the State of New York.

Dr. Woodward spent 11 years with Wilson Learning Corporation heading up the development of new products in the areas of leadership-management and quality-service. In 1988 he was made a Wilson Fellow. In 1989 Dr. Woodward left Wilson Learning to head up his own consulting firm, Woodward Learning International, Inc.

Dr. Woodward has also worked in the Training and Development Division of 3M Corporation and taught at the University of Minnesota. He is currently at work on a series of booklets and e-learning modules dealing with the key issues of organizational and personal change.

Dr. Woodward works and speaks nationally and internationally on the subjects of change, consulting, learning, and humor. He is coauthor of the book *Aftershock: Helping People Through Corporate Change* and author of the award-winning video-based program "Working Through Change." He is also the creator of the Change Readiness Profile. His book, *Navigating Through Change* is currently available through McGraw Hill.

Dr. Woodward lives in Minneapolis with his wife, Mary. He enjoys swimming, reading, photography, classical music, and hiking the Superior Hiking Trail on the North Shore of Lake Superior.

Mark J. Tager, M.D.

Mark Tager is president and CEO of WorkSkills-LifeSkills, a training and publishing company serving the corporate marketplace with products and services that help people achieve great performance. He received his medical degree from Duke University and trained in family practice at Oregon Health & Science University. Early in his career, he served as medical director of Electroscientific Industries and as director of health promotion for Kaiser Permanente in Portland, Oregon. In addition, he wrote a syndicated newspaper column titled "The Wellness Bag," and produced early cable health programming for ABC Video Enterprises.

Dr. Tager founded Great Performance, Inc., a communications company that he ran for ten years before it was acquired by Times Mirror/Mosby. The company featured training programs in wellness, stress and change, leadership, disease management, and occupational health and safety for consumers and professionals.

As senior vice president of business development for Mosby Consumer Health, he was responsible for establishing programs in partnership with leading domestic and international companies such as the American Heart Association, Bristol-Myers Squibb, and Eli Lilly.

After leaving Mosby, Dr. Tager served as president of Risk Data, a division of HNC Software in San Diego, and as a consultant to a variety of medical device, e-health, nutrition, and training-related companies.

As an entrepreneur, Dr. Tager has built successful businesses and managed high-performance teams. As a consultant to large corporations, he has served as an effective change agent and visionary. As an educator, he has created dozens of wellness-oriented training programs for consumers and providers. As a physician, he understands the unique dynamic that is at the center of health and well-being. Dr. Tager has coauthored five additional books: *PowerSource: How People and Organizations Can Transform Stress and Manage Change*; *Whole Person Healthcare*; *Planning for Wellness*; *Designing Effective Health Promotion Programs*; and *Working Well: Managing for Health & High Performance* (with Marjorie Blanchard).

Dr. Tager lives outside of San Diego with his wife, Carol, his children, James and Marissa, and their English springer spaniel, Patches.